© 1986 Residenz Verlag, Salzburg and Vienna
Printed in Austria by F. Sochor, Zell am See
ISBN 3-7017-0448-1

SALZBURG

The beautiful city

Text
WILFRIED SCHABER

Photography
WERNER SCHNELLE

English translation
GAIL SCHAMBERGER

Residenz Verlag

The Residenz Fountain. Engraving by Paul Seel, c. 1665

Salzburg — A Contradiction

Salzburg is a favourite destination for tourists, but not only because of the festivals which are gradually dividing the whole year into seasons of varying length and importance; the attraction lies in the peerless charm and beauty of the town itself.

This beauty has found many admirers, not least the traveller and explorer Alexander von Humboldt, who wrote in 1804 that memorable sentence: "The regions of Salzburg, Naples and Constantinople are to me the most beautiful on earth". That was a hundred and eighty years ago, and much has changed since then. But evidently today's visitor still finds here something that very few towns can offer.

Opinions have not always, however, been exclusively enthusiastic; Salzburg has been faced with sharp criticism or even rejection. Wolfgang Amadeus Mozart wrote to his father from Munich in 1779: "... I swear to you upon my honour that I cannot stand Salzburg and its inhabitants — I mean the native Salzburgers; ..." Thomas Bernhard has condemned the town and its inhabitants, Peter Handke has voiced repeated criticism, and many artists see the Old Town merely as a "baroque desert of stone".

A survey of enthusiastic and critical comment makes it apparent that aversion is directed primarily at the inhabitants, perhaps owing simply to personal experience. But how can appreciation of the town be reconciled with dislike of its inhabitants?

A milieu has a lasting effect on those living in it, shaping them to a specific and unmistakable type. The elemental characteristics of a place — environment, landscape, climate — are constants which also mould the people. And art is the materialisation of a specific situation in life, the interpretation, always fresh, of the *genius loci*. Is it not, then, the key to the character of a place and its inhabitants? Is there not bound to be something in common between the two? Here we come up against a contradiction intrinsic to Salzburg, an enigma as yet unsolved.

Our primary aim in this book is to trace the artistic traditions and landmarks that constitute this incomparable townscape. How far conclusions may then be drawn about the Salzburgers is for the reader, the visitor to this lovely place, to decide. Just one question to start with: is Salzburg in fact the town of the Salzburgers? Does it really belong to them? In summer, one is perfectly entitled to doubt this, for the cafés and restaurants, the museums, the squares, the streets and the back lanes, and even the finest apartments have been taken over by "foreigners". The town has become in effect a gigantic stage, with the Salzburgers as, at best, supernumeraries, employed to man the box-offices ... Is this phenomenon peculiar to our time; have the Salzburgers succumbed to the economic allurements of the tourist industry, or is there in fact a historical constant to be detected here, even if in a modernised form?

For centuries, the court of the archbishops held its celebrations here, erected magnificent buildings and made spectators of the citizens. The prince-archbishops came from abroad; so did the artists: for them the town was a stage, with the scenery provided by the aristocracy. The citizens had little part in all this; they grudgingly sold their houses to the archbishop when the noble sector of the town required space for impressively-architectured squares. The cathedral precincts expanded at the expense of the burghers' town; even in those days, scarcity of accommodation was acute.

The town "lives" (in all senses of the word) from its singular beauty, which it is the purpose of this book to demonstrate. Sightseers flock to Salzburg every year in their hundreds and thousands. What is its attraction for tourists, those restless nomads of our time who, synchronised with school and factory holidays, flee the bleak deserts of the big cities to invade this oasis, thirsting after sentience and beauty? The 20th century traveller, generally with a thoroughly rationalised everyday existence, seeks stimulation for the deep-down emotional levels of his personality. He is moved and excited by wild unconquered mountain ranges, by the sea — and by places of pervasive charm. He seeks out foreign parts with an aura of "romance", which transport him, without the aid of "history", back to a vague distant past. "Romantic" places are idyllic, magical, mysterious, distinguished by abundance and variety and a strongly defined aura. All this applies to Salzburg. The densely-built old streets create "atmosphere", inducing the unremittingly heightened emotional state sought after by the modern traveller. Salzburg's monuments, and indeed the whole townscape, meet these emotional and visual expectations. The area around St. Peter's appeals to the romantic side of the observer, the Cathedral precincts with their façades and squares represent clarity, unapproachable splendour and order, and the monuments of the baroque age contribute plasticity and mobility to the town's vital image. The visual attractions are so many and so various that the visitor in a hurry has soon seen and experienced "enough". And then "to suck the honey out of the stone and the oil out of the hardest rock" (thus Guillaume Durand, in the 13th century, allegorised the trouble taken over interpretations of the Christian liturgy) does not interest the modern tourist. If this kind of understanding is to be achieved, Salzburg's distinguishing features require attentive and even unconventional observation and commentary, far removed from any high-flown ideas on art. The pictures and the text of this volume are intended to provide pointers.

Reflections on the "essence" of Salzburg

SALZBURG BETWEEN ROCK AND RIVER

The countenance of the town is determined essentially by its hills — the Mönchsberg-Festungsberg ridge, the Kapuzinerberg and the Rainberg — set against the background of an Alpine panorama. These hills were at one time islands in an ice-age lake which filled the whole basin up to the mountain ranges, and they attracted settlers early on in history. After the prehistoric waters had dried up, the Salzach, coming from the mountains and seeking a route through the Alpine foreland, managed to force its way between the hills to flow on freely to the North. Until it was regulated in the 19th century, the river meandered at will through the countryside, its path through the town being prescribed by the natural limit formed by the rock, so that river and rock fashioned the town. The caves in the Mönchsberg, perhaps already consecrated as chapels by the early Christians, may have been formed by river erosion in prehistoric times. Within the town boundaries, undisturbed alluvial sand lies four to six metres underground; the town is built, if not quite on sand, then on a bank of gravel which forms approximately a semicircle with its western end at the Müllner Tor (Mülln Gate) and the other at the Kajetaner (St. Cajetan's) or Schanzltor, at the eastern face of the Nonnberg.

Hence the Old Town does not stand on firm ground, since gravel banks are subject to changes when, according to season, water brings or removes alluvial deposits. Where humus has settled, water may suddenly channel its way through. Contingency and disorder prevail; the form of the gravel bank changes unresistingly, dictated by the caprices of the weather far up in the mountains.

Thus the foundation of the town is somehow unstable, and its northern boundary, the river bank, is constantly changing course. If it is true that places derive their essence and atmosphere from their boundaries and walls — "A boundary is not that which marks the limit of a thing; a boundary is where the essence of a thing begins." (Martin Heidegger) — then Salzburg, standing on insecure ground and bordered by a changeable river, must be characterised by a singular "disorder", by an existential "indeterminacy".

Peter Handke has provided some thought-provoking epithets; he has called Salzburg "the city of disorderly pedestrians", and said that "mustiness" is one of its characteristics. "Did you ever lose your footing in the woods, while climbing a mountain for instance, and reach through the underbrush to grab a rotting tree trunk? Precisely because your hand meets with no resistance, you feel for a moment as if it were gone . . . I've often had a comparable feeling when coming into this city", says a painter in Handke's "Across".

Here dubious characteristics of the town are revealed, to which many succumb ("Some say the city puts them in a bad mood") and to counteract which others have created great works.

The only unchanging thing in Salzburg has been the cliff that surrounds the town to the south like a high wall. The support given in other towns by a firm foundation has been supplied here by the vertical rock face of the Mönchsberg. It was in the caves in this mountainside, where the primordial forces of the earth are still present, where alone in the area of the Old Town security and stability were to be found, that the hermits of the early Middle Ages discovered the secret of nature which meant to them the presence of

God. Is it surprising, then, that the town's Christian founder was called Rupert (Lat. rupes=rock), and that he consecrated his foundation to St. Peter, the rock on whom Christ built his Church? Mystic associations between the name and the character of the town are touched upon here; legend has it that Rupert, who had first settled in Seekirchen, came at the behest of an inner voice to the rock in Salzburg to found here his episcopal church.

This rock, the Mönchsberg, is really a flat ridge, a bank of rock, a left-over piece of land. "The ridge of the Mönchsberg is not straight, but recapitulates the meanders of the Salzach below. The mountain consists of the delta rubble deposited by the river as it emptied into the great lake that was there thousands of years ago. The rubble was deposited evenly and rhythmically in layers that can still be discerned in the slightly tilted striped pattern which runs along the whole length of the mountain, and is accentuated in winter by the blown snow in the grooved stripes and by the serried rows of icicles. The rubble — ranging in content from small pebbles to fist-sized stones — is held together by a light-gray block of limestone which with its abrupt promontories, needles, sharp edges, and cracks gives the Mönchsberg its jagged, craglike character. Where the pebbles have fallen out of the limestone, innumerable craters seem to darken the rock. The layer of humus at the top is thin, and the roots of the trees (for the most part, beeches and oaks) grow right through the often porous shelf of rock below it". (Peter Handke, "Across").

Building can become quite unintentionally a means of understanding; the people of Salzburg have made the basic form of their houses resemble the solid block of the Mönchsberg. In the houses of the Old Town — cubic, sharply defined, with flat roofs, following the lines of the narrow streets — one can recognise the ridge of the mountain. The individual houses have been combined into rows until they are indistinguishable one from another, none having distinctive characteristics. Thus unwelcoming, isolated "reefs" of houses grew up, with continuous expanses of wall, encouraging no communication with the environment. The walls are flat, unrelieved by oriels or balconies, without ornament or colour. The predominant shade was grey, until in recent years a commission prescribed more bright colours for the Salzburgers, to cheer the place up.

The style of these Salzburg houses has often been attributed to Italian influence, but it would be more accurate to speak of local necessity, for the solid box-like aspect of the rows is indigenous to Salzburg, a materialisation of the forms existing in the town's environment. The row of houses rising from the narrow lanes imitates the extended ridge of the Mönchsberg. The roads have dug themselves like ancient gutters into this conglomerate of closely-packed houses, and the river seems to have forged its way anew through the town, leaving a shallow layer of gravel between the houses as it went. Throngs of visitors push through the narrow streets like detritus. This "city of disorderly pedestrians" is not suited for crowds in motion; mass meetings are held exclusively on the Residenzplatz, which looks like an artesian well, with the fountain in the centre jetting up from the water-bearing gravel foundation.

On a subsoil like this, there can be no vegetation of any great age. Venerable trees are conspicuous by their absence in the Old Town; the mighty ginkgo on the west side of the University Church is "erratic", a curiosity remaining from the former botanic gardens.

Many of the houses have a sunken look, stuck in the ground with no visible base; the palace walls, on the other hand, soar confidently on their massive plinths. The buildings of this town have no firm foundation in the shallow ground, but a kind of stability has been achieved by building the houses up against each other, producing a remarkable effect of "suspension". This "suspending" of buildings "by cords from heaven" was not always an empty metaphor. The dome of the Church of St. Sophia was described as hanging on a golden cord, and the vaulting of the Gothic cathedrals seemed to the people of the time to be anchored in the clouds. Sacred buildings did not always have to be erected laboriously, against gravity — the idea that they once floated out of the air, borne by angels, was perfectly familiar. "For it is a very modern concept that the will which went into creating a building was simply that of an artist" (Erhard Kästner).

It is the background of the Mönchsberg that lends stability to the buildings; architecture and cliff are morphologically related. The domination of the long flat wall surfaces, not even appreciably interrupted by openings, is another peculiarity of Salzburg's building tradition. Here, too, the cliff face was the unintentional model, the building a rendering of the environment in accordance with the "genius loci".

"YOU ARE RULED BY THE SHADE"

The mighty precipice towering above the town obstructs the light and lengthens the shadows; the Old Town is quite literally "overshadowed" by the mountain. Sundials show the time only in the middle of summer, when the sun is at the zenith. Nevertheless — or perhaps because the movements of the shadows were so conspicuous — a Salzburg printer published in 1719 a highly erudite, anonymous work on "Schattenwerfer" (shadow-casters), as sundials were termed therein — an unusual epithet, but understandable, considering the situation of the town. Archbishop Leopold Anton, Baron von Firmian (1727—1744), a collector of watches and all kinds of chronometers, had many beautiful sundials constructed. The Museum Carolino Augusteum houses a few particularly fine examples. A sundial is also portrayed on Firmian's portrait medal of 1728, with the significant inscription: "Me sol, vos umbra regit" (I am ruled by the sun, you by the shade).

One 18th century innkeeper in the sombre Gstättengasse was not content to defer to this verdict, and right in that part of the street where the sun never penetrated, he hung above his door a radiant golden sun, to attract customers to the "Gasthaus zur Sonne" in the shadowy lane.

GENIUS LOCI

The ancients believed that particular places, springs, trees, groves or parts of the countryside with some special feature were inhabited by guardian spirits. Ancient myths tell of these divine beings, whom no mortal might behold with impunity; he would be afflicted with blindness or madness. These powers, usually invisible, were believed to exist within material objects, from which they were inseparable and on which their lives depended. They were local guardian spirits, but they could, apparently, be driven out by the destruction of their abode. Countless examples could be mentioned of Christian missionaries cutting down sacred trees or filling in venerated springs, and remaining nonetheless unpunished. Were these, then, not real powers, but mere images of man's own psyche? The Greeks endowed them with a definite human shape; to the Romans they were *numen*, an efficacious divine power, and later *genius loci*, the guardian spirit of a place. "They must have been associated with material things in a manner which is not as simple to define as our intellect would like and as the old legends represent" (Walter F. Otto). In the eerie, slithering, amorphous nature of the snake, Roman belief found an appropriate image for its idea of the chthonian origin of the genius loci.

Building in such places was undertaken in accordance with the genius loci, the "opposite number" with whom man had to come to an agreement, if he was to live in harmony with the world around him. It is that harmony, hard to define, that we admire in old towns and villages, that we notice in the lie of a farmstead on a hillside or in the way in which characteristics of the landscape are reflected in the architecture of men.

The old part of Salzburg is an outstanding example of this harmony between countryside and town, between nature and art. Respect for the genius loci does not by any means, however, entail imitation of the ancient models; to protect and preserve the guardian spirit is to achieve a rendering of its nature and its character in ever-differing historical situations. This is possible only if the town is seen as an individual, evolved, living organism and not as an abstract space for the "blind" forces of economy and politics to operate with free rein. The punishment dealt by the genius loci for the destruction of a place does not consist in a demonstration of its power, but in its disappearance. A place loses its identity when the buildings no longer bear any relation to the landscape or to the town as a whole, when the town centre has ceased to operate as the heart of the community, when to be "without shelter" has become a common symptom.

Solari's Cathedral building and the Gothic Franciscan Church, with the tower of the Nonnberg Convent Church in the background

Residenzplatz with the Cathedral and the Residenz, the cathedral arcades and fountain →

The Cathedral with the square in front, at the far left the Glockenspiel

The many-windowed choir of the Cathedral with the high altar

The row of chapels in the south nave of the Cathedral

Horse-drawn cabs on the Residenzplatz

The inner courtyard of the Residenz

The "Schöne Galerie" in the Residenz with the niche above the fireplace for the "Jüngling vom Magdalensberg"

The Franziskanergasse with the Small Festival Hall in the background

The high altar in the Franciscan Church

In the courtyard of St. Peter's Monastery

← The towers of St. Peter's Church

St. Peter's Monastery precincts with the Small Festival Hall in the background

In St. Peter's Cemetery

The Franciscan Church with the dome of St. Peter's and the Chapel of St. Margaret

Hohensalzburg Fortress above the city towers →

The ornamental horse-pond on the Kapitelplatz

The Herrengasse

The "Goldener Saal" in the Fortress

In the Fortress

The towers of St. Peter's Abbey

View to the north over the town from Hohensalzburg

St. Erhard's Church in Nonntal

The abbey of the Benedictine nuns on the Nonnberg

Portal of the convent church on the Nonnberg

In the convent church on the Nonnberg

The houses on the Waagplatz and the Mozartplatz and the Church of St. Michael, with the Capuchin Monastery in the background

Private chapel in the "Andretter" house at no. 4, Mozartplatz

Arcaded courtyard in Georg Trakl's house, no. 1a Waagplatz

The Mozartplatz

St. Florian's Fountain on the Alter Markt

The Alter Markt

The Café Tomaselli on the Alter Markt

The Getreidegasse

The "Grünmarkt" (University Square) with Mozart's birthplace

The Collegiate Church

St. Peter's and the Small Festival Hall

The Felsenreitschule

The "Wilder Mann" fountain and the Collegiate Church

The former court stables and the ornamental horse-pond — today the Large Festival Hall

The Neutor (Riedenburg side)

The Getreidegasse with the tower of the Bürgerspital Church of St. Blasius

The Bürgerspital (burgher's hospital) at the foot of the Mönchsberg cliff

The Gstättentor (Gstätten gate)

View towards the Mülln Church

← The Old Town from the north-west

St. Mark's Church with the Gstättengasse on the right

The Augustinergasse in the suburb of Mülln

Salzburg from the north-west

View from the Mönchsberg over the suburb of Riedenburg, with the Rainberg and the Untersberg →

The Mirabell Gardens

The marble staircase in the Mirabell Palace

The stone fencers at the entrance to the Mirabell Gardens

Vestibule in the Mirabell Palace, looking on to the statue of Pegasus

In the arcades of St. Sebastian's Cemetery

Statue of St. Mark in Wolf Dietrich's mausoleum in St. Sebastian's Cemetery

The tanners' houses in the Imbergstrasse

Holy Trinity Church, in the background the Mirabell Palace

Panorama of the town, looking south, with the Fortress and the Untersberg

The Hellbrunner Allee

The Palace of Hellbrunn

Great hall with frescoes in the Palace of Hellbrunn

The "Roman theatre" in Hellbrunn

Pond in Hellbrunn

The "Monatsschlössl" on the Hellbrunnerberg

The Palace of Leopoldskron

Klesheim Palace

The pilgrimage church of Maria Plain

The dome of the Collegiate Church and the Capuchin Monastery

← Hohensalzburg Fortress at dusk

Holy Trinity Church and St. Sebastian's Church, with the suburb of Gnigl in the background

Domes and towers in Salzburg

The Origins of Salzburg — Early Monasticism

The Mönchsberg provides not only a visual but also an intellectual focus. Speculation about Salzburg's origins finally comes to rest at the cliff wall; for here in these caves, one reflects, the history of Salzburg might well have begun. Origins are a fascinating study, since they determine the later development and the resulting character of a town.

We can trace the origins of Salzburg through a "profane" version of history, constructed from a chronological framework of dates. However, the further one goes back into the past, the scantier are the sources, especially of positively authenticated information. A further opportunity for retrospection is offered by the "historia liturgica" — ecclesiastical history, as believed and experienced. The Church's calendar of feast-days recapitulates the entire course of spiritual and religious history, seen in a universal context; it reflects (taking into account the important role of local saints, according to diocese) the whole "company of saints", whose commemoration days are also reliable dates in profane history. From early times, biographies of local saints have supplemented the information in the calendar and provided useful historical data.

Quite a different approach to history and origins can perhaps be opened up by a typological view, just as far removed as liturgical history from the chronological method. Typological thinking works by making analogies between various fields, using one to illuminate and clarify the other and discover its meaning. This search for association of meaning can link the most distant things, affording a glimpse of the "Wechselleben der Weltgegenstände" (Goethe: relationships between things in the world). It can discover in nature prefigurations and models, and it recognises a common cause behind similar behaviour in nature and in human beings.

There are certain kinds of region with a strongly-marked topography, a distinctive genius loci, giving rise to related behaviour of animals and humans; one of these is a cave-riddled cliff above a river. In the literature of ancient times, the cliff and the cave represented a refuge for the meek, for the doves. And those who take the dove — which "lives solitary in the desert, for it loves not the tumult of men" (the *Physiologus*, c. 200 A. D.) — as their model in nature

"petra refugium" — the rock is a refuge.
Emblem by Henrik Engelgrave, 1654

do likewise: those are the monks. Dove and monk, falcon and knight are pairs in antithesis: the one symbolising the contemplative, the other the active life. For the doves, which have "secret nests and homes in the hollow rock" (Vergil, *Aeneid*), the cave is a refuge from the falcon; so do monks find in the hollow cliff shelter from the dangers of the outside world. "The (turtle) dove likes to seek solitude; and it behoves the noblest servants of Christ to seek solitude" (the *Physiologus*).

THE ROCK IS A REFUGE — PETRA REFUGIUM

This 17th century baroque emblem could stand as a symbol with the motto "petra refugium" for Salzburg's early history. The picture of the cave-riddled cliff above a river, with a dove fleeing before a falcon, was further illustrated by its publisher, the Jesuit Henrik Engelgrave, with appropriate quotations from ancient and Christian literature telling of the cave as a refuge for suffering. On the door of a cell in the novices' quarters of St. Peter's Monastery, the emblem is aptly (and with significant allusion to the patron saint) captioned "petra refugium".

The Bavarian historian and humanist Johannes Turmair, called Aventinus (1477—1534), recognised, in his "Bavarian Chronicle" (written in 1520, printed in 1566), this "refuge motif" dominating the Mönchsberg cliff in Salzburg, and attempted a historical verification. His linking of the cave chapels ("catacombs") with Eugippius' martyrology of Maximus ("more than 55 were thrown down the cliff . . . as is still shown and related today") is, however, inaccurate, being based on the confusion of the place-name Joviaco (Schlögen, on the Danube) with Juvao (Salzburg). In the 17th century, the historians of St. Peter's, especially the Mezger brothers in their "Historia Salisburgensis" (1692), retained the "refuge motif" — not from concrete historical knowledge, but probably in the main through their knowledge of biblical and non-biblical typology — and associated the martyr legend with it. But from this same century dates also the tradition of a "habitaculum" of St. Rupert in the Chapel of the Holy Cross in the Mönchsberg cliff.

This new tradition heralds a more critical historical understanding, and the "refuge motif" becomes associated with the much better authenticated figure of St. Rupert, the "founder of Salzburg".

ST. SEVERIN

During the precarious years following the death in A. D. 453 of Attila, king of the Huns, there appeared in the Roman Danubian province of Ufernoricum a saintly man called Severin. This province, which included the town of Juvavum (Salzburg), extended from the banks of the Danube to the main Alpine ridge, and from the Vienna Woods to the Inn. The vacuum left by the disintegration of Hun supremacy was breached by the Germanic tribes. Rome had the province cleared, especially the endangered places on the Danube, and the Latin-speaking town population was evacuated to Italy. Severin, a Roman, who appears to have been a high adminstrative official before his call to Christianity, organised the retreat of the Romans from the imperilled Danube frontier. His travels brought him to Salzburg, and his pupil Eugippius, who wrote Severin's biography in the year 511, tells of the miracles he worked here:

"Thus it came to pass, near a town called Iuvao, one day in summer, when the people came to the evening service in the basilica and there was nowhere a fire to light the candles; neither were they able to make fire in the accustomed way, by striking stones together, and the hour advanced so far, while they were striking iron against stone, that the time for the evening service was past. But the man of God knelt down upon the ground and prayed fervently. And forthwith, before the eyes of three priests who were there, the candle which St. Severin held in his hand began to burn. By its light the evening service was held in the usual fashion, and thanks were rendered unto God for everything . . ." (Chapter 13)

"It happened that a woman from the same place, tormented by a long illness, was lying near to death. Preparations were already made for the funeral, but her relatives allowed the voice of faith to subdue their lamentations, and they laid the almost lifeless body of the sick woman in front of the door of the saint's cell . . ."

Through his prayers, Severin restored her to life. ". . . but on the third day after her recovery, the woman began work in the fields, according to the custom of the land." (Chapter 14)

There are several parts of this report which are worthy of note as far as Salzburg is concerned. The miracle of the candle took place in a "basilica" nearby, on the outskirts of the town; three "spiritales" are mentioned. Following linguistic usage of the time, these expressions indicate a monastery church and a community of monks. Severin seems to have lived in one of the "cellulae" of this monastery. Eugippius' report testifies to the existence in fifth-century Salzburg of a community of monks with a church, but the location of such a church is still not known. If one takes into account, however, that in this troubled century which saw the collapse of Roman supremacy, the towns in the plains were depopulated and the inhabitants sought once more, as in Celtic times, the safety of the highlands, one does not necessarily have to look for this monastery outside the boundaries of *modern* Salzburg. At the time when Rupert came to the town (696), only the Nonnberg terrace was inhabited, and this was perhaps so even in Severin's day (around 470). In that case, the monstery, in the area of the present St. Peter's Monastery, could well be described as being "near the fortified town" (oppidum). The only place that could be fortified at that time, anyway, was the Nonnberg terrace, so "oppidum" could in fact refer to the hillside town on the Nonnberg, the "castrum superius" of the 8th century.

Arcosolium (so-called "martyr's grave") in the Maximus Chapel of the cave chapels in St. Peter's Cemetery. Lithography by Georg Pezolt, 1871

Eugippius' account is up to now the only evidence of an Early Christian Salzburg; no undisputedly Early Christian finds have yet been excavated. The reason for this absence of finds could be the fact that Salzburg was never a garrison town, that it never harboured soldiers, who were usually the first to carry Christianity out to the boundaries of the Roman Empire. The monastery (beside which one would have to assume a community church) could have been exclusive to the upper classes of the Roman population — a common circumstance in those centuries. Finally, the possibility should also be considered that Christians had withdrawn from the Danube regions, which had become unsafe, into the security of Salzburg, in the interior of the province.

It cannot as yet be established how long this monastery of Severin's day was in existence. But when Rupert came to Salzburg more than two hundred years later, he found the Monastery of St. Peter (and the Church of St. Martin, on the Nonnberg) already there.

THE ITINERANT BISHOP HRODPERTUS

Hrodpertus, Bishop of Worms and descendant of a powerful family, was related to both the Merovingians and the Carolingians. Contrary to strict canonical law, he left his bishopric, probably during the 680's, and moved to the court of the Bavarian Duke Theodo in Regensburg (Ratisbon), where he instructed court society in the Christian belief. Then he undertook a journey to Noricum, in search of a suitable place to continue his work. He travelled down the Danube as far as the Late Antique bishopric of Lorch, right on the frontier to the troubled territory of the Avars; there he turned back and went to Seekirchen on the Wallersee, where he built a church. His sojourn at the Wallersee was brief: "When he learned that there was a place called Juvavum (Salzburg) on the River Ivarus (Salzach), where there had stood of old many wondrous buildings, now almost in ruins and covered by forest, he asked the Duke for this place, that he might deforest and clear it." He arrived in Salzburg in 696. The Duke bestowed upon him the town and the upper fortress for his new foundation, along with generous portions of the surrounding lands in the Salzburggau, the Attergau and the Traungau (Gau = district). Twenty brine-pans in Reichenhall, vineyards around Regensburg and abundant pasture and woodlands formed the nucleus for what was to become the extensive territory of Salzburg.

Rupert founded the convent on the Nonnberg, with as its first abbess his niece Erentrudis, whom he had brought with him from home after a short visit in 714/15. He was also the founder of the Cell of Maximilian in Bischofshofen (771/12), where he built an oratory and cells for monks. The sources give exact terminological data concerning the founding of these two monasteries, whereas Rupert's services to St. Peter's Monastery are described only with the words "cleansing, renovation and restoration". This makes it quite clear that Rupert must have found an already existing community of monks at the foot of the Mönchsberg cliff. He merely renovated their living quarters and erected a church, which he consecrated to St. Peter. This brings the origins of the monastery up to a date closer to that given for the foundation by liturgical history (582).

Around 716, Rupert must have returned to settle in his home district of Worms, for in that year one Bishop Martinian was ordered by Pope Gregory III to organise the Bavarian church. Rupert, whose name is not mentioned in this connection — he was never, in fact, bishop or abbot in Salzburg — must at this time already have returned to his ancestral seat in Worms, where he died soon afterwards.

The motives behind Rupert's activities in Salzburg are still altogether unexplained; historical research has to rely on mere assumptions. Why did Rupert abandon his bishopric in Worms? According to the canon law of the time, a bishop was obliged to remain in his hereditary seat. It would seem that Rupert turned his back on Worms because of "political" problems; but it must also be considered as a possibility that he was only an itinerant bishop, without a specific see. One may assume that the Bavarian Duke Theodo then, in accordance with the Germanic proprietary church system, which allowed him to appoint church dignitaries on his own land, suggested that he set up a new bishopric in the eastern part of the realm. Rupert's first visit was in fact to the bishopric of Lorch-Lauriacum. According to Roman canon law, the founding of a new bishopric by the ordination of a bishop would have been possible here without judicial problems, but the dangerous proximity to Avar territory may have proved a deterrent. Perhaps Rupert came to Salzburg because of its sheltered position at the edge of the mountains, and because of the evidence of Christianity remaining amongst the Roman population of the Salzburggau, whose spiritual centre seems to have been the ancient Monastery of St. Peter. Duke Theodo's plans for a bishopric around 716 came to nought, for reasons unknown, and it was not until 739 that Boniface, called the apostle of Germany, elevated Salzburg to the status of bishopric and consecrated Johannes first Bishop of Salzburg.

The church in Salzburg assumed under Rupert the character of a monastery church, with the old Monastery of St. Peter as its focal point. It was supported by the resident Roman population in the area between Salzburg and Pass Lueg — those who had not left the province in the 5th century after the collapse of the Danube frontier. In the 8th century, the majority of the monks of St. Peter's still went by Roman names, in clear contrast to the minority with Bavarian/Germanic names. Salzburg still retained this monastery church atmosphere under Virgil, and it was Archbishop Arno (Arn) who, with a well-educated body of secular clergy, first achieved the conditions necessary for the administration of a newly-created bishopric. The Duke of Bavaria, too, emphasised Salzburg's new-found importance by erecting a palace here, probably in about 702. The Duke's son Theotpert ruled here over a partial duchy, and his son Hucpert held the seat until 725. The Langobard King Ansprand and his son Luitprand lived in exile for nine years with Theotpert, probably in Salzburg.

Rupert's activities on behalf of the Duke of Bavaria were responsible for that antithesis between the monastery and the administrative centre of the prince-archbishops, between "solitudo" and "mundus", which was to determine — and frequently to trouble — the course of the ensuing centuries. The ancient monastic community was not yet capable of fulfilling the secular duties of a bishopric. Despite the dissimilarity of their duties, the secular clergy (canons) and the monks lived together for almost three hundred years, until the separation of the community and — more painful still — of the property, in 987. St. Peter's Monastery remained throughout the centuries true to its monastic ideal, whereas the archbishops and canons became involved in "secular things" — in disputes with emperor and state. The community of canons was dissolved in 1514, and after secularisation in 1803, the ruling power of the prince-archbishop became a thing of the past, his duties being reduced to the pastoral domain, as in the time when the bishopric of Salzburg was founded, so that, apart from the spiritual seclusion of the monastery, he should lead the Christian community in a church covering the whole province.

ECCLESIA PETENA - AQUILEIA AND SALZBURG IN THE DARK AGES

The Church of Petena — this puzzle, too, is bound up with the early history of Salzburg. Before considering Virgil and Arno, we should sketch out the problem of the "Church [or town] Petena, now called Salzburg", into which merges, in recent decades, the tangle of uncertainty that once surrounded Rupert. This takes us back to pre-Rupertian days.

In documents dating from the period in which Salzburg was raised, under Arno, to the status of bishopric (798), the name "Petena" is mentioned several times, allegedly as the oldest name for the Salzburg church. In the ensuing centuries, this designation disappears completely from documents, later to be "unearthed" once again by sixteenth-century Humanists.

The question of "Petena" is connected with the "uncanonical founding" of the bishopric of Salzburg. The foundation of any bishopric required an ancient title; the place should at one time (perhaps in the Christian Late Antique period) have been the seat of a bishop, or have acquired the right through transference of the title from an extinct bishopric. Although Salzburg had been a Roman *municipium*, it had never been a bishopric of Noricum. Duke Theodo and Rupert had chosen their site well, as far as the topography goes, but a legal title for the bishopric they planned to found in 716 seems to have been wanting. The simplest explanation of the mysterious "Petena" would, then, be the transference to Salzburg of the title from the obsolete bishopric of Petena in Istria, providing a "canonical basis" for the archbishopric under Arno. Other explanations make use of names, connecting Petena-Salzburg with the Roman Bedaium on the Chiemsee, or with Rupert's Seekirchen on the Wallersee.

Perhaps the solution lies in an early link between the ancient Istrian bishopric of Petena and the pre-Rupertian monastery of St. Peter. For the monastery which Rupert found in existence had either survived from the days of Severin, or been founded — or perhaps merely restored — by an itinerant bishop.

We must, however, take into account effects of Aquileian church politics in our own region; and it is almost certain that here is a link with the name of Petena. In 579, a synod was held in Grado, the "Nova Aquileia" moved here because of the sheltered situation of the island; one of the bishops taking part was Marcianus, from Petena in Istria. In this same period, another Marcianus (allegedly not the same one) was buried in a privileged spot, beside the patriarch Elias, in Sant'Eufemia, the cathedral of Grado. A recent (and only verbal) conjecture links this latter Marcianus with our own region. This is indeed a tempting hypothesis, since the inscription on his grave tells that he was a bishop for forty-three years, forty of them as an itinerant bishop (missionary) in foreign parts. To judge from the inscription, he seems to have died abroad, but been buried in 578/579 in this eminent place. His travels, therefore, would have been undertaken during the years 538/39—579. If it should turn out that this itinerant bishop Marcianus (was his home see Petena in Istria?) visited the Aquileian metropolitan district north of the Alps, the problem of Petena would be solved. This could be the basis of a tradition in the Monastery of St. Peter that it was "founded" by a bishop from Petena. The monastery's great age did not give it sufficient right to be elevated to archbishopric under Arno; the existence of a bishop in early days had to be proved — perhaps that very Marcianus (from Petena?). As soon as the status of archbishopric had been achieved, this old tradition disappeared from the documents — understandably, since Aquileia might otherwise have brought ancient claims to bear. Indeed, a dispute did break out, under Arno, over the metropolitan boundary to Aquileia; this was settled by Charlemagne, who fixed the limit as the River Drave.

The theory is further supported by the fact that the art of illumination in 8th-century Salzburg is strongly influenced by manuscripts from the Late Antique period, and even a sixth-century illuminated manuscript from the region of Upper Italy/Ravenna/Aquileia must be assumed as the model for the illustrations in the Cuthbercht Codex and the Codex Millenarius in Kremsmünster. Moreover, there were found in Salzburg "remains of biblical volumes which were written long before his [Rupert's] time, but which could already have been in Salzburg in his time . . ." (Bernhard Bischoff; e. g. a fifth-century fragment of the Gospels). It is understandable that even an itinerant bishop had to equip his foundations with the necessary liturgical volumes, which he would bring with him from his home see.

These conjectures bring us right up to the period of the liturgical date for the founding of St. Peter's (582). It happens frequently, of course, that the "historia liturgica" preserves data that are "correct" according to profane history, but which later become confused with other persons and events. For Salzburg, Rupert was a kind of focus for all traditions that had anything to do with its origins. Rupert's period is now defined with certainty, but this does not invalidate the liturgical date for the founding of the Monastery of St. Peter — from another point of view, it gains new and unsuspected significance.

Which monuments of this early age have been preserved in Salzburg? If one ascribes the "two-chamber building" in the centre of St. Peter's, discovered during excavations, to the Rupertian period, then all that remains is a carved stone block which today serves as a support for Roman funeral chests (containers for urns) in the vestibule of St. Peter's Church. This block is decorated with very roughly executed spiral vine ornamentation stemming from a trifoliate centrepiece. This type of vine decoration appears first in the age of Constantine, and is familiar from mosaics, especially those of Aquileia. The extremely rough Salzburg version of it, refracted through intermediate stages of provincial craft, indubitably belongs to the Late Antique period; the date may be taken as 5th or 6th century, although it cannot be proved that the stone was part of a Christian building.

VIRGIL FROM IRELAND

It is possible that traditions of Late Antique period Christianity were preserved in the pre-Rupertian monastery of St. Peter. Rupert, Bishop of Worms, restored this community in the spirit of the Merovingian-Frankish Church, and after his return to the Rhineland, Boniface (whose real name was Wynfrith), a zealous Anglo-Saxon, visited Bavaria in the service of the Holy See, in order to reform this young church once again, this time in accordance with his "Roman" ideas.

Boniface set great store by the precise use of Latin, since he considered grammatical accuracy in the priest's formulas for consecration to be a condition of the efficacy of the sacraments. The "Bavarian" Latin of an indigenous priest at a baptismal ceremony, incomprehensible to Boniface, occasioned a dispute in which Virgil, an Irishman, became the Anglo-Saxon's opponent. The Bavarian priest, whose command of Latin was scant, had baptised the child "in nomine patria et filia et spiritus sancti" (in the name of the fatherland, the daughter and the Holy Ghost). The Pope decided this argument against his legate Boniface, on the grounds that what he interpreted as heresy was merely ignorance of Latin on the part of a Bavarian priest. Now Boniface brought a much more serious accusation against Virgil, saying that he was spreading a false doctrine "of another world and other men who lived under the earth". The Anglo-Saxon was apparently familiar only with the image of the Earth as a disc. But according to the ideas of that time, this disc was surrounded by ocean, so the assertion of the existence of "antipodes", of men on the other side of the Earth, conflicted gravely with the Church's teaching that Christ, by his death on the Cross, had redeemed all men of the line of Adam. Those living on the underside of the Earth could not, because of the dividing ocean, be of Adam's line, and had not, therefore, been redeemed by Christ. Virgil was summoned by the Pope to Rome, to vindicate himself. From this precarious situation he emerged once again victorious; he pointed out that the Earth was spherical, thereby proving the descent of all men, even the antipodes, from the line of Adam.

In these two men, Roman legalism and that Irish scholarship in which ancient learning persisted came into conflict, with Bavaria, and possibly Salzburg, bearing the brunt of their fundamentally different philosophies of life. After the Frankish Rupert, Virgil the Irishman was to direct the church in Salzburg, which Boniface had organised according to Roman ideas. Under him and the Bavarian Agilolfing family, the bishopric of Salzburg became large and important, but with the downfall of this dynasty, the memory of the erudite Irishman disappeared, and Salzburg was developed along new lines by Archbishop Arno. Even the early days of Salzburg offered no opportunity for the slow and steady growth of traditions, for the town was from the start the scene of completely different spiritual ideals. In the 8th century, the seed was already sown for that attitude to life shown by the inhabitants, of dealing with events by "taking cover". A social survey of 1816, a thousand years later, says of the Salzburgers: ". . . they show a kind of shyness towards anyone who is not a native. The reason may well lie in the many changes of government which took place within a short time . . . They withdraw into their own domestic circles, and avoid any political discussion . . ."

Who was in fact this courageous Irishman who, through his erudition, put even the papal legate in his place? In the period after 739, when Boniface had established the four Bavarian bishoprics, Regensburg, Freising, Passau and Salzburg, "at that time, when Odilo was Duke of Bavaria, subject to Pippin, King of the Franks, there came to the king a very wise and learned man (vir sapiens . . . et bene doctus) called Virgil, from the island of Ireland . . ." It must have been in 743 that Virgil came to the court of the Frankish king with a group of Irish monks. A year later, he was already active in Bavaria (dispute with Boniface), and after the death of Johannes, first bishop of Salzburg (746/47), Virgil became abbot of the Monastery of St. Peter. Two years later, in 749, he was consecrated bishop.

It has not yet been established with certainty where Virgil originally came from. It is certain that he was a monk in the monastery on Iona, an island off the west coast of Scotland, where St. Columba founded the first Scottish community of

The Maximus Chapel of the cave chapels in St. Peter's Cemetery.
Engraving, 1661

monks. But Virgil (Irish: Fergil) is reputed to have been abbot in a famous monastery in central Ireland. The following extract from Irish annals: "Fergil, called the Geometer, Abbot of Achaid Bó [Aghaboe], died in Germany in the 30th year of his bishopric", corresponds to the actual year of his death, 784. The opinion also exists, however, that this source refers to another person of the same name.

In Ireland, also called the "Isle of Saints", a flourishing monastic life had developed in the early Middle Ages. The spiritual heritage of ancient times had always been cultivated here; many of the Irishmen who travelled on the continent were "scholars", and Virgil, too, had the status of a "sage". For the Irish monks, life on earth represented a journey at the end of which was the true homecoming, so they regarded the "pilgrimage for Christ" as a physical realisation of the homelessness of man on earth. They sought ascetic fulfilment in exile, in their journeyings through foreign lands. The idea of missionary work was not foremost in their minds, but took shape along with the political consciousness of the Carolingian realm. It is most significant that Bishop Virgil did not fulfil his missionary duties to the Slavs and the Avars with the zeal and energy deemed by the Agilolfings (or perhaps the Franks?) necessary for their political designs. The *bon mot* has even been coined, that in the time of Rupert the Frankish-Bavarian eastern mission got as far as Bischofshofen, while in the same period Islam conquered the whole of North Africa and half of Spain.

The pilgrimages and monastic foundations of the Irish were not aimed at territorial gain and mass baptism, but at seclusion and asceticism, the conquest of spiritual territory. It was nonetheless Bishop Virgil who, through his talent for organisation, established the wealthy and excellently organised diocese of Salzburg. He pursued an uncompromising policy of proprietary churches, which frequently brought him into conflict with the aristocracy, accustomed as they were, under Germanic custom and law, to founding proprietary churches and "family" cloisters on their own lands, thus combining the saving of their souls with the furtherance of private policies. Virgil refused to consecrate such foundations, successfully insisting that he alone should appoint priests and monastic superiors, and that the bishop of Salzburg should be the recognised head of all ecclesiastical instiutions in the diocese. Shortly after his death, there were in the ecclesiastical province of Salzburg (bordered in the west by the Inn and in the south and east by the Mur and the Drave) sixty-seven episcopal proprietary churches and eleven episcopal proprietary monasteries, such as Zell am See, Au and Gars on the Inn, Elsenwang and Zell by Kufstein. Besides these, there was still a considerable number of proprietary churches belonging to the aristocracy, but the bishop was their highest authority. This administrative centralisation necessarily led to the weakening of the old-established aristocracy; already making itself felt here is the strong hand of the episcopate, which also in later centuries managed to prevent the establishing of proprietary cloisters by the aristocracy. How often was the indigenous nobility faced with the alternatives of declaring itself in opposition to the bishopric or else placing itself and its property under the protection of the church, in which case the property devolved on the Salzburg church as soon as the family died out, if not before. This "strong hand" policy, which began with Virgil, was responsible for the colossal territorial expansion of the bishopric, which centuries later, along with the secular rights of the rulers, led to the formation of an ecclesiastical principality.

Virgil organised the church in Salzburg like a gigantic "monasterium" (possibly modelled on the large Irish monasteries with hundreds of monks), in which each individual was assigned specific duties. It is interesting to note that even long after Virgil's day, Salzburg was still called a "monasterium", in contrast to the three other Bavarian bishoprics. The numerous episcopal proprietary churches and the "farming" monasteries in the country formed strong points in a network of communications covering the entire province. Ecclesiastical and economic functions were closely linked; wherever the ground had been cleared for a church settlement, Christianity could flourish. This outstanding infrastructure created by Virgil during his thirty years in the diocese of Salzburg may have been one of the reasons for Salzburg's elevation to the status of archbishopric under his successor Arno.

Virgil had a powerful ally in building up the diocese — the Bavarian dukes of the Agilolfing family. Their generous gifts of land contributed decisively to the fact that Salzburg was, even before Arno, the richest and economically strongest of the Bavarian bishoprics. The founding of this influential centre in the south-eastern part of the Frankish realm was indeed not devoid of political motives. The retrospective reports (from the years around 870) on the Salzburg Slavic mission give an idea of the true reasons seen in the light of recent research. It is possible that the ruling Franks were already interested, at the beginning of the 8th century, in gaining control of the region immediately north of the Langobards (Carinthia and southern Pannonia), which was subject to Avar and Slavic tribes. At that time, isolated missionaries, not necessarily delegated by Rupertinian Salzburg, may have been sent into this region. Even in Virgil's early days in Salzburg, priests travelled to the country south of the Alps, although they were apparently not sent out directly from Salzburg, and the Carantanian mission was only gradually transferred to Virgil's Salzburg. Probably it was mainly because of Tassilo III's victory over the Carantanians (772) that by the time of Virgil's death the political annexation of Carantania (Carinthia) to Bavaria was completed. Evidence that the plans were more extensive, that the warlike Avars were also to be included in this pacific campaign, is provided by an alphabet closely related to ancient Turkish runes, contained in a manuscript attributed to Virgil. For it would be in keeping with our idea of this scholarly Irishman that he should "invent" for the mission to the Avars what was a necessary basis for true mutual understanding: a script appropriate to their language, in order to "translate" the substance of Christian belief. Virgil had created this instrument more than a hundred years before the "Apostles of the Slavs", Cyril and Methodius. The reason why it was not adopted, or did not achieve the breakthrough which made the "Glagolica" of Methodius the script of the Slavic Church, possibly lies in the reluctance of the Church of Rome at that time to preach the Gospel in the vernacular. At any rate, in the 9th century the mission from Salzburg lost altogether its area of southern Pannonia (on Lake Balaton and on the lower courses of the Mur and the Drave) ". . . when a Greek called Methodius undermined in sophistic fashion, with newly-devised Slavic characters, the Latin language and the teaching of Rome as well as the official Latin script, and caused the entire people to despise the services and Gospel teachings of those who celebrated in Latin . . ." (from the history of the conversion of the Bavarians and the Carantanians).

The literary work containing the ancient Turkish runic alphabet and also the antipodean doctrine which so annoyed Boniface is alleged to be an excerpt taken by Hieronymus, Doctor of the Church, from the work of a legendary Christian geographer called Aethicus Ister. The whole work was unmasked as an early mediaeval literary "forgery", nevertheless going back to ancient cosmographic traditions. The actual author is said to have been Virgil, and although this cannot yet be proved, the work must have been written in his vicinity, since there is evidence in it of "Hibernian" Latin, typical Irish turns of phrase. There is also a book on numbers which is ascribed to Virgil, but perhaps this was the Abbot Fergil, "the geometer", whose identity with our bishop is now considered uncertain.

In the latter half of the 8th century, Tassilo III, Duke of Bavaria, had espoused the political designs of the Frankish kings in the south-east of the realm. He wished, however, to enlist the aid of the Slavs and the Avars in increasing his power and his influence, and it is even said that he intended creating a Bavarian royalty. Tassilo married Liutpirc, daughter of the Langobard king Desiderius (c. 765), and achieved the climax of his power with his victory over the Carantanians (772). At this time, he was extolled as the "new Constantine", conqueror of the infidels, and represented through his family tie with the Langobards a serious threat to his cousin, Charlemagne. His sudden downfall followed shortly afterwards. Indicted before the annual assembly for non-participation in campaigns and for conspiring with the Avars, he was condemned to death in 788, but then his life was spared, and he was relegated to a monastery. The members of his family also spent the rest of their days in cloisters, and thus the Agilolfing line came to an end.

Virgil of Salzburg had worked closely — all too closely — with Tassilo. The enormous cathedral building — the largest north of the Alps at the time — had perhaps been intended for the coronation and funeral celebrations of the Bavarian kings. Virgil did not live to see Tassilo's downfall, but he did fall prey to the "damnatio memoriae", the effacement of his memory. For it cannot be otherwise interpreted, the way in which, with the death of this eminent man who had contributed so much to the greatness of the diocese of Salzburg, every memory of him was obliterated. Sixty years after his death, his grave in the south wall of the cathedral had already been forgotten, and a chapel was built over it, regardless. His successor, Arno, was a faithful follower of the Frankish "faction", as Charlemagne's realm appeared to be; the Bavarian star had set, and with it the memory of Virgil, whose spiritual significance is only gradually being rediscovered.

ARCHBISHOP ARNO — SALZBURG BECOMES A METROPOLIS

Arno, a Bavarian, was abbot of the monastery of Saint Amand, near Elnon in Belgium, when he became Virgil's successor in 785. It is uncertain whether he owed his appointment to Tassilo or to Charlemagne. At any rate, his period of office in Saint Amand had furnished him with the best connections in the Frankish court, especially to Alcuin of York, the superior of Charlemagne's Palace school, with whom he remained on friendly terms during his years in Salzburg. A wealth of correspondence bears witness to this friendship; Alcuin affectionately called the black-haired Arno "aquila" (eagle). Numerous manuscripts came from the various cultural centres of Charles' realm to Salzburg, to be copied here. Under Arno, the library was augmented by 150 volumes — an enormous number, considering that even an experienced scribe took several months to copy a book.

Bishop Arno survived Tassilo's downfall in 788 unharmed; it would seem that Charlemagne placed the greatest trust in him. There are various reasons for supposing this, and it has even been suggested that Charles placed under Arno's authority as abbot the noble Agilolfing ladies who were confined to a convent. In a Salzburg necrology, a Liutpurga and a Cotani are mentioned in the Convent of St. Amandus; these are almost certainly Tassilo's wife and daughter, although this has not been proved. The emperor repeatedly availed himself of the bishop's services for diplomatic missions; Arno frequently travelled at Charlemagne's behest throughout the realm and to the Pope in Rome, and still found time to complete the work begun by Virgil in Salzburg. He continued the mission to the Carantanians, although not with any great zeal; Alcuin had to admonish him to fulfil his pastoral duties in Carinthia.

During one of his sojourns in the Papal See, as envoy of Charlemagne, he was promoted by the Pope to the rank of archbishop, and Salzburg became the metropolis of the Bavarian Church (798). Arno directed the diocese of Salzburg for thirty-six years, twenty-three of those as archbishop, and until 808 he was still entrusted with the administration of his monastery in Saint Amand. He died in 821, aged eighty, and was buried in the "gate tower crypt" he had built in Virgil's cathedral.

Archbishop Arno completed the work started by Rupert and Virgil in building up the Church in Salzburg, and crowned it with the distinction of metropolis. The Agilolfing family and Charlemagne had done much to promote the new bishopric, and its rise shifted the focus of importance from Bavaria to the south-east. It is more than surprising that the older centre of Regensburg had to take second place to Salzburg. Under the Agilolfings, the determining factor may have been their intention of founding a royal palace here; for Charlemagne, Salzburg's geographical position was decisive, since in the early 9th century the ecclesiastical province of Salzburg extended to Lake Balaton in the east and to the River Drave in the south. In 811, the Drave was declared by Charlemagne as the boundary between Aquileia and Salzburg, after Aquileia had considered Salzburg's mission to the Slavs an "interference" in ancient rights.

VIRGIL'S CATHEDRAL, SACRED BOOKS AND THE TASSILO CHALICE

From modest beginnings, Salzburg was elevated to surprising greatness by three men — Rupert the noble Frank, Virgil the Irish scholar, and Arno the shrewd tactician from Bavaria — plus a self-assured ducal house and the Carolingians. The wealth of the diocese is represented by Rupert's attribute, the salt cask, while the model of the church, Virgil's symbol, refers to the artistic achievements of those years.

"In the year of Our Lord 767, Virgil began the building of a church magnificent in size", we read in the annals of Salzburg. In 774, when the remains of St. Rupert were carried with ceremony from Worms (or, according to other sources, from St. Peter's Monastery in Salzburg) to the newly-completed cathedral, this building "of astonishing size" was consecrated. Excavations in the area of the early baroque cathedral have made possible a reconstruction of its ground plan, enormous by the standards of the time, 66 metres long and 33 metres broad. Nothing has been definitely established about the vertical projection, since up to now only a small part of the area has been accessible for examination. Virgil's cathedral could have been a basilica, with a triple nave, columned or pillared arcades, and on the east side an apse shaped like a clover leaf, giving the building a "memorial" character (was Rupert's grave in the crypt underneath?). The parts of the ground plan hitherto excavated, however, make it open to a quite different interpretation: as a hall with an apse to the east and spacious annexes to the north and south of the eastern part (so-called pastophories). These annexes would have been extended as far as the west façade (in order to form "porticos" on the exterior for ducal tombs?), so that the pattern of the foundation walls would be hard to distinguish from that of a basilica. These complex questions cannot be elucidated without further investigations.

Virgil's cathedral was certainly richly ornamented with paintings and sculptured stone. The sheer size of the church — a miracle, it seemed, then — and its decoration, the costly fabrics and the gem-studded gold liturgical vessels may have afforded the people of the time intimations of the celestial.

We know about the lustrous gold paintings from the demolition (1181) of the cathedral which had been destroyed fourteen years earlier, for then Virgil's grave in the south wall was rediscovered, along with "ancient golden paintings". His likeness bore the legend: "Virgil erected the temple in splendid fashion".

Under Archbishop Arno, the new "orientation" of the Bavarian metropolis and its now close bond with the Frankish kingdom became evident also through the building programme. Arno added to Virgil's cathedral a "gate tower", which may have replaced a previous atrium, and whose vaulted lower storey was vestibule, crypt and burial-place all in one. This is the only way to interpret the report that Arno was buried in 821 in the "crypt" he himself had built at the west side of the cathedral. His epitaph reads: "O traveller, if thou ask who built this crypt, know that I completed the work in my own lifetime . . ."

During the Carolingian period of architecture, the gate tower developed into a new architectonic prototype. In its direct and predominant association with the main church building was symbolised the proprietary church system, the close interlinking of state and church, emperor and clergy — the gate tower was the domain of the supreme secular lord, the emperor. Consequently this architectonic motif forfeited its significance after the time of the investiture struggle, the conflict between emperor and pope over the right to appoint bishops. Thereafter, gate towers were no longer built, and existing ones were altered. The cathedral erected by Archbishop Konrad III (begun in 1181) shows none of these "lordly" motifs; this late Romanesque cathedral was the first to be *exclusively* a metropolitan church. Of course, Salzburg remained only for a short time influenced by Frankish political friction, for its remote situation in the south-west of the kingdom later prevented the cultural influence of the emperor's court from gaining too much importance, and served to further its own special territorial development. In the 8th century, the town had indeed been the residence of the Agilolfings, and the ducal palace at the "porta" — the passage (still in use) beside the small Church of St. Michael — constituted a counterpoise to the bishops' stronghold around the cathedral. However, the dukes of Bavaria were resident in the town for only about ninety years, and after Tassilo's downfall, the palatinate declined in significance. In 1291, Archbishop Konrad IV was even able with impunity to demolish the building, which had been renovated under Barbarossa. The "Romanischer Keller" (Romanesque cellar) on the Waagplatz, still accessible today, was part of this imperial palace of Frederick I.

Whereas the cathedral precincts were built on a generous scale, the spiritual and secular power of the princes being given palpable expression in splendid architectural style, the little Church of St. Michael (formerly the palatine chapel) still bears witness to the days when the archbishop of Salzburg was not yet a prince, and was opposed by secular power in the person of the duke palatine. But the "village church", chapel-like character of St. Michael's bears witness also to the early retreat from Salzburg of the representatives of secular power, relinquishing this territory to the Church. Looking from the Mozartplatz towards the Residenz and the Cathedral, one can readily imagine this historical process.

Besides the cathedral, a few other churches remained from the days of Virgil and Arno — for instance, there was a baptistery on the site of the present Franciscan Church and a Church of Our Saviour in the part of the town across the bridge. But the deciding factor in our image of early mediaeval Salzburg is the distribution of building in the area between the Cathedral and the Mönchsberg.

The cave-chapels in the rock were already consecrated by Virgil; the Chapel of St. Gertrude, for instance, was originally dedicated to St. Patrick. We know Virgil's cathedral, but not the "beautiful church" (dedicated to St. Peter) which Rupert built after he had renovated the Monastery of St. Peter. Neither can we form a picture of that episcopal church indispensable to Johannes, the first bishop of Salzburg (739). Its foundations could still, however, be concealed in the remains of the walls of Virgil's cathedral. Although the "two-chamber building" discovered during excavations in the centre of St. Peter's Church dates from the early Middle Ages, and the later church was built, significantly, around this *locus sacer,* it is indeed difficult to recognise in this small building the "ecclesia formosa" of Rupert. The remains are reminiscent rather of an oratory or a tower such as the early abbots of Montecassino are said to have built. But the monks' quarters, renovated by Rupert, must undoubtedly be sought in the area of St. Peter's. Of course, we cannot expect to find monumental remains of this early monastery, since most buildings were of wood, and probably only the church was built of stone.

Our notions of Rupert's activities in Salzburg are still strongly marked by hagiographical tradition. Was it perhaps these late legends that made the little tower-like oratory in the centre of the later monastery church into the "ecclesia formosa"?

The area at the foot of the Mönchsberg cliff appears to have served as a burial-ground since the 6th century, when the Bavarians settled there. Archbishop Arno built here a "crypt church" dedicated to the patron saint of the cemetery, Amandus. Remains of this building have been excavated; together with the "two-chamber building", it formed the nucleus of the later monastery church. From the Arno period of the monumental building that took place in Salzburg, there survives in St. Peter's Monastery an impressive, beautifully-fashioned marble capital, decorated with loosely-woven interlaced creepers. The nearest comparable monuments with this type of "vegetal" interlacing ornament are to be found in Carolingian Milan.

A so-called "family of churches", with cathedral and baptistery, oratories and cemetery church, was a salient feature of the town in early centuries. The canons lived in the cathedral monastery, which stood on the Kapitelplatz, and very early on, the monks detached themselves from the community which lived according to a mixed Columban/Benedictine rule, to lead their secluded life, dedicated to the monastic ideal, by the cemetery under the cliff. Whereas the cathedral canons attended to the "secular" duties of the bishopric, such as administration and pastoral work, the monks devoted themselves primarily to contemplative occupations. They produced the books, and may also have made the liturgical vessels.

One would expect that artistic and cultural development might be traced without interruption in a monastery, establishing long-standing traditions. In the Monastery of St. Peter, however, exactly the opposite is true: over and over again, ready-made "styles" from outside were adopted. This dependence on external tradition is particularly evident in the manuscripts. Under Virgil, the script is strongly influenced by Saint Denis (near Paris) — sober and austere, with occasional Irish/Anglo-Saxon idiosyncracies. Arno's episcopate represents for Salzburg "yet another importation of a ready-made script, developed elsewhere together with its traditions of illumination" (Bernhard Bischoff). Arno's monastery of Saint Amand had all at once become a model for the script practised in Salzburg. Under his successor Adalram (821—836) "[yet another] new style makes a sudden appearance on the Salzburg scene . . . that cannot be explained from any existing Salzburg tradition" (Bernhard Bischoff). This time, a prominent teacher from Mondsee

Carolingian marble capital in St. Peter's

was appointed, and he transplanted the "calligraphic" scriptorial traditions of this monastery to Salzburg. It is indeed odd that constant stimulus had to come from outside. On the other hand, through its very lack of formal grounding and its absence of tradition in creative art, Salzburg offered favourable conditions for "foreign" artistic concepts to flourish, sometimes quite exceptionally well, since the "import" encountered no resistance from any strongly developed local traditions.

Nevertheless, throughout all the stylistic alterations of the script, a Salzburg style is recognisable — unadorned, sober, austere, of such extreme clarity that it could have been written on squared paper. The strict, ordered intellectuality expressed by this script lasted until the decline of the local scriptorium in the 13th century.

Another peculiarity of early Salzburg should be mentioned: the interest in foreign alphabets and scripts. Nowhere else have so many examples been preserved: Greek, "Old Turkish" runes, Gothic, and a secret cipher intrigued the Carolingian scribes. Can this be interpreted as a reaction to the many foreign influences at work here? Do these alphabets represent an attempt to overcome such influences?

The illumination of manuscripts, too, presents a heterogeneous picture. Whereas under Virgil the Irish/Anglo-Saxon traditions of ornamentation are mingled with drawings of human figures in Late Antique style, and the figures of the Evangelists are strongly outlined on the light-coloured background of the parchment, while the ornaments are more substantial (Cuthbercht Codex), Arno brings to Salzburg traditions of the Frankish Palace school. The representation of the months in a codex illuminated under his auspices follows closely in its "impressionistic" style the models of the Late Antique period, and reflects in its colour and vitality something of the splendour and abundance of the art of illumination in the Palace school.

Writing was for the monks an ascetic exercise; "the heart [should be], as the parchment, cleansed of dirt and coarseness, so that the heavenly script may find upon it a good ground" (Hildebert de Lavardin) and ". . . the Devil suffers as many wounds as the scribe writes words of the Lord" (Cassiodor).

In the Carolingian period, the Salzburg scriptorium was exceptionally productive. There is evidence of up to thirty scribes (counting a good many apprentices), of whom more than ten would have been trained and experienced "scriptores". Arno augmented the library by over 150 books; the steady growth of the stock of books already came to an end, however, under Archbishop Liupram (836—859). Of course, the production of books under Arno demanded a wealthy and well-organised economic basis, considering that the parchment for one codex required the skins of more than 200 goats, sheep or calves.

We know less about the goldsmith's art in early mediaeval Salzburg, but three of the major examples from this period are linked with Salzburg: the "Rupertuskreuz", the Tassilo chalice and the so-called "Älterer Lindauer Buchdeckel".

The Rupert cross in the Cathedral museum is of English manufacture, from the first half of the 8th century, and was probably brought to Salzburg by Virgil. The beauty and the workmanship of this monumental cross, of chased and gilded sheet copper (from the south of England) over wood, makes it quite unique in the art of this early age. A "naturalistic" vine (symbol of Christ) entwines in strict symmetry the stem of the cross. Heraldic pairs of four-legged beasts and waterbirds nibble and peck at the buds and the clusters of grapes. The southern sense of form is evident in the naturalistic drawing of plants and animals, and only the sides of the cross, with their insular style of interlacing, and its gem-like "stones" of molten glass, point to the northern origin.

The Tassilo chalice in Kremsmünster Abbey is also connected with Salzburg art. The inscription "Tassilo dux fortis — Liutpirc virga regalis" (Tassilo, mighty ruler — Liutpirc of royal line) could indicate that it was made as the wedding chalice for the union of the Duke of Bavaria with the Langobard Princess Liutpirc (c. 765). This exceptional relic of early mediaeval art also combines elements from the most varied cultures. The interlacing and details of the medallions strike an insular note, the decoration of the node is taken from Late Antique models, and the iconology has been labelled as "Greek". Despite the heterogeneous artistic traditions juxtaposed in this work, the end product is a homogeneous and magnificent creation in which "in the midst of the independent mobile ornamentation of the drawing... the medallion figures [seem] to materialise as characters expressing individual personalities" (Wilhelm Messerer).

The older "Lindauer Gospels Book Cover" (in the Pierpoint Morgan Library in New York) is covered with a large cross and decorated with animal and human figures. As with the Tassilo chalice, many varied techniques have been used — niello, cloisonné, chip carving and almandine inlay. The shining gold surface of the cover gains added lustre from the turquoise green of the enamel and the red of the almandine. The book's great religious significance in the early Middle Ages is thus palpably expressed, its message being vital to man — the Gospel of Jesus Christ.

Salzburg has been postulated — though not undisputedly — as the place of origin of all these masterpieces. Firstly, it was the principal episcopal see in Southern Germany, and the insular elements were easily accounted for through Virgil and his fellow-monks from Ireland; secondly, there was also a ducal seat here, and Tassilo seems to have spent long periods with his court in Salzburg. His marriage with Liutpirc may help to explain the Upper Italian/Langobardic elements in Salzburg art. But it was above all Salzburg's "scenic" quality which made such achievements possible. The town offered a grand setting for foreign art, and arranged it all in fresh "ornamental" contexts. The aim was not that of complete fusion, but of harmonious co-existence of heterogeneous elements, based on a concealed sense of order, an "art of arrangement".

From Bishop Virgil's day there remains a monumental document in which "order", in a practically liturgical and also in a metaphysical sense, is demonstrated: this is the Confraternity Book of St. Peter's. For the intercessions during mass, there were written down in this book the names of all the living who had some special close connection with the community, and next to them the names of the dead, who were recorded in the "Book of Eternal Life". The Confraternity Book was a mirror of this heavenly Book of Life, a symbol of the timeless community of the Church. It formed a link between the living, in a particular historical situation, and the dead — the patriarchs and the prophets of the old covenant and the apostles and martyrs of the new, the kings and dukes, bishops, abbots, monks, secular priests, deacons and anyone else closely associated with the church. All these "ranks" are represented by lists of names arranged in two columns: the living and the already departed.

This work, laid out in such an orderly fashion, could correspond only for a short time to the actual situation, since as soon as the bearer of one of the names died, he had to be entered in the column of the dead, and his name removed from that of the living. As the names increased in number, the complicated business of additions and erasures led to confusion and disorder. The church later took to recording only the names of the dead, in necrologies. Virgil's Confraternity Book collocated the timeless community of the Church, but its ordered continuation was doomed to failure because of the temporal nature of the register of the living.

There was in this area, besides Salzburg, another notable monastery producing works of the highest artistic quality — namely that of Mondsee. But the art of this monastery shows, in contrast to Salzburg, a strongly individual character, a marked ability to assimilate foreign influences, so that works such as the Tassilo chalice (which had been attributed also to Mondsee), with its harmonious if "exotic" juxtaposition of various elements, would have remained alien to it. The peak period of Salzburg's art in the Carolingian age was soon past; the loss of the mission territory in Pannonia to Methodios, around 870, was a serious blow to the archbishopric. But the foundations already laid were durable; in arduous times and under weak rulers, the archbishopric may have lost something of its glory and importance, but not of its powers of renewal. The 10th century brought attacks by the Hungarians, and Archbishop Theotmar fell in the Battle of Pressburg (907), in which the Bavarians suffered an annihilating defeat. In these precarious years, the archbishops of Salzburg sought refuge in the mountains, and erected in Zell am See, around 926, a large church which could serve the reigning archbishop as a "church in exile". Under the Hungarian assault, Charlemagne's "Ostmark" collapsed, and Salzburg now lost its Slavic mission territory as well. The work of reconstitution after the crushing defeat of the Magyars on the Lechfeld did not meet with great co-operation on the part of the new Ottonian line of emperors, who transferred their attention to Saxony. Only an inner renewal could restore the archbishopric to its former importance.

Power and asceticism — the greatness of Salzburg and its flourishing monastic culture

The tenth century brought, throughout Europe, a strengthening of the movement towards asceticism. Reformed monasteries, such as Cluny, in Burgundy, and Gorze, in Lorraine, revived monasticism through strict observance of the rule of St. Benedict. By way of Regensburg, which soon adopted the reforms of Gorze, Salzburg also came into contact with this revival. Added to the austerity of monastic discipline was the safeguarding of the monastery estate against the laity and secularised bishops. The return to a simple and strictly ordered life increased also the economic power of monasticism; the monsteries, in addition to royalty and the episcopate, became a determining factor in the empire.

In Salzburg, the monks were from the start closely associated with the bishopric, and until 987 the bishop had been at the same time abbot of St. Peter's. This tradition derived from the monastic origin of the Church in Salzburg. With the increasingly secular duties in the diocese, the pastoral work in the parishes and the administration of the extensive territory of the bishopric, there accrued for the monks tasks which could be performed only in contravention of their monastic ideals. A separation of the communities had become inevitable, and this was effected in the year 987: the monks of St. Peter's submitted to Benedictine rule, dissociated themselves by a legal act from the bishopric, and were given as abbot Titus, who was to govern the reformed monastery. Concomitant with the relinquishing of the union with the bishopric was the provision of property and legal rights which were to assure the monastery's economic independence. But this provision came to only a fraction of what magnanimous donors had at one time given to Salzburg's monastery church. The monastery received only as much as was absolutely necessary for its existence. This scant provision of property from the formerly joint estate was repeatedly, in later centuries, a bone of contention between St. Peter's Monastery and the cathedral chapter. What had, at the time of the separation, appeared adequate to the monks of St. Peter's for the realisation of their ascetic ideals was to seem decidedly skimpy in later ages, when the strict monastic life was no longer the exclusive aim and the splendid court of the archbishops was constantly before their eyes. They did, however, manage to gain over the cathedral chapter the right if burial (of great economic importance) and the privilege of the monastic community to go in processions directly in front of the prince-archbishop. This latter right of "precedence" was designed to express the pre-eminence of the monastery over the cathedral chapter, and its more ancient privileges. For an age which thought in terms of strictly observed hierarchies, this right of precedence was the expression of an order hallowed by age, and it was only after protracted litigation that the cathedral chapter acquired it by an exchange, in 1657.

At the time of the monks' separation from the bishopric, they were given a large monastery church of their own, the walls of which were found during excavations under the present building. It was built to the pattern of a basilica, with a triple nave and a crypt on the east side. This first monastery church may have incorporated in its eastern part the adapted St. Amandus Church of Bishop Arno. The "two-chamber building" from the time of Rupert was situated right in the middle of the nave. Whether it was preserved as an architectonic "relic", a "memorial" of the church founder Rupert, or whether it was demolished. cannot yet be established. At all events, the ground plan shows a significant and manifest consideration for this *locus sacer*, this holy place.

Archbishop Hartwik (991—1023) provided for the new requirements of regular canonical hours in the cathedral by erecting a large chancel, 27 metres long, in place of the apse built by Virgil. The report that he modified altars seems to apply to this reconstruction of the eastern end of the old cathedral. It was not until a century later that Archbishop Konrad I (1106—1147) added "extremely high" west towers to the venerable building. Until the catastrophe of 1167 — when the Emperor Frederick Barbarossa is said to have had the town set on fire because of its loyalty to the pope — the old cathedral remained standing; its nave dated back to Virgil, its gate tower to Arno, and the long chancel was added by Hartwik, in accordance with the new liturgical requirements.

The history of the building of the old cathedral shows a development parallel to that of the bishopric of Salzburg. Virgil laid the "foundations", which sheltered in the crypt the remains of the founder, Rupert. His cathedral determined, by its width and by the length of the atrium and the nave, all the later alterations up to the time of the destruction of the old building. For four hundred years, his successors merely made additions and extensions. The bishopric developed along similar lines: the basis was already laid down in Carolingian times, and the ensuing centuries simply expanded on this nucleus of land by means of gifts and acquisitions. The old hierarchy, too, according to which the emperor was the sovereign lord, able to create bishoprics with the consent of the pope, remained in force in the old cathedral until the 12th century, in the link between the gate tower and the church. At the height of the investiture struggle, however, the Archbishop of Salzburg finally took his stand on the side of the pope, and the destruction by fire of the old cathedral, reflecting the breakdown of the long-standing union of emperor and Church, put an end to the old architectural ideas. The new building, begun under Archbishop Konrad III (1177—1183), symbolised, with its wealth of towers and cupolas, a "celestial stronghold", the "celestial city". The metropolitan church was now exclusively the spiritual and liturgical centre of the archbishopric, which was at this time about to become an independent territory, a principality in its own right. Under Archbishop Hartwik, Salzburg acquired the right of coinage, the right to hold a market, and jurisdiction; thus the beginnings of a gradual transformation of the mediaeval sovereign state into the modern form of the territorial state are rooted in the 10th century. The difficult years of the investiture struggle, from the time of Archbishop Gebhart (1060—1088), one of the most prominent champions of the papal faction, only furthered the transformation of the archbishopric into the later principality. As a defence against the power of the emperor, the fortresses of Hohensalzburg, Hohenwerfen and Friesach were extended, the frontiers of the province fortified and the road communications improved. The archbishopric developed into a well-defended minor state.

The revival of a strong ascetic movement along the lines of the Gorze reforms led also to the flourishing of the scriptoria. After the rebuilding of the monastery churches (Nonnberg had also been reconstructed around 1000), the liturgical books were rewritten and profusely ornamented. The style of these follows the traditions fostered in those monasteries from which the reforms had been adopted. St. Emmeran's, in Regensburg, played the major role in transmitting the new Ottonian style, followed later by the monastery of Prüfening.

It was also by way of Regensburg that the markedly Byzantine style of manuscript illumination arrived in Salzburg, a style which has frequently given rise to the assumption of direct connections with the Byzantine Empire (perhaps via Venice). In the second half of the 11th century, a series of manuscripts with costly illumination was created in St. Peter's Monastery, one of them being signed "Custos Perhtold". These miniatures are richly underlaid with gold leaf and framed with architectonic motifs such as pillars, walls, pinnacles and arches, which lend to the scenes from the life of Christ the stability and authenticity of architectural constructions. Here the Byzantine influence is manifest in the hieratic austerity and consistency of the figures, in their calm presence, free of movement and haste. Some seventy years later, in the 1140's, the so-called "Walther Bible" (now in the Monastery of Michaelbeuern) appeared, with pictures from the Old and the New Testaments giving an emotional, even anecdotal turn to the account of events. The height of the art of illumination in the 12th century is marked in 1160 by the Antiphonary of St. Peter's (Austrian National Library, Vienna). Lavishly decorated with pen-and-ink drawings and miniatures in gold leaf and bold, brilliant colour, this work bears witness to the excellence attained by the Salzburg scriptorium on the eve of the catastrophe which befell the town in 1167.

This century's mural painting also followed Byzantine models; the frescoes in the niches under the nuns' choir-loft in the Nonnberg Convent Church (c. 1150), depicting various saints, give an idea of the kind of painting that originally graced Salzburg's churches.

The goldsmith's art, likewise, shows the highest artistic quality in the middle decades of the 12th century. The so-called "ministerial chalice" from St. Peter's Monastery (now in the History of Art Museum in Vienna) is an artistic creation of silver gilt, rock-crystal, niello and precious stones, its bowl held by twelve embossed figures of the prophets. Round the rim runs a text in Kufic script, repeating four times in Arabic the declaration "the dominion is God's".

Besides the monks of St. Peter's, there were, right from the earliest days of the Church in Salzburg, the cathedral canons, who also lived as a community and undoubtedly had a scriptorium as well. We know little about this in the years following the separation from the monks, and it is not until the 12th century that this scriptorium of the cathedral monastery comes more clearly to our notice. In 1122, Archbishop Konrad I introduced the Augustinian rule into the cathedral chapter, and this tightening of discipline in the canonical life served as an incentive for a productive scriptorium, which has become known only in recent years. Unlike the Monastery of St. Peter, it had no older tradition to build on, and had to adopt ideas from outside. Because of this, the newest monastic reforms of Hirsau and Klosterrath took effect in the cathedral monastery, and the most progressive currents of thought established themselves in the cathedral library. Archbishop Eberhard I (1147—1164) had been a monk in Prüfening and Abbot of Biburg, and had studied in Paris for some years. The pen-and-ink drawings in the necrology he instituted in 1150 show a "modern" style modelled on such drawings as may be found in Paris, within the sphere of influence of the new Cistercian monastic reforms.

A comparison of the styles of drawing and handwriting in the monasteries of the cathedral and St. Peter's would demonstrate the difference between their respective spiritual climates. The cathedral monastery, entrusted with the pastoral and secular duties, reacted more sensitively to innovations; its script, not yet settled, is more open and uneven. The script of St. Peter's is more hieratical, formal and regular, and vies with its Byzantine models in the gold and the vivid colour of its illumination. These two "schools" are joined in the 12th century by the Nonnberg Convent with books of its own. The two monasteries may also have had their own mural painters, who worked in Chiemsee, Salzburg, Friesach, Lambach and Pürgg. The necessity of distinguishing the share of the two Salzburg "schools" in the execution of these frescoes, and of examining their influence on the scriptoria of other monasteries and suffragan sees has been recognised only in recent years.

The introduction of Augustinian rule in the cathedral called for the rebuilding of the monastery (on the Kapitelplatz). At the same time, St. Peter's also felt the need for new monastery buildings. Abbot Balderich (1125—1147) built, between 1130 and 1143, the monastery church which is substantially the one still standing today. In that part of the church accessible to the laity (in front of the former rood altar), the bays are separated by the Saxon system of two columns alternating with one pillar, and to the east of these, in the monks' choir, there are pillars only. In the middle of the church stood the rood altar, and behind it, raised on piers over the so-called "crypt", was the pulpit. Remnants of the paintings and frescoes are still visible on the walls of the main aisle, on one of the columns and in the side aisles. Balderich's basilica had a flat raftered ceiling, and the clerestory windows were placed lower than the present ones.

The late Romanesque portal as we see it today is the result of various alterations. The tympanum and the lintel date from the latter half of the 12th century; the reveal was not completed in this form until around 1244.

St. Peter's is the part of Salzburg in which one can best capture the atmosphere of the town's mediaeval history. The cliff and the cemetery take us back to the beginning of the Christian era, and in the "cave chapels" in the Mönchsberg we can trace the monastic, hermitic origin of Salzburg. These cave chapels, of course, look quite different today. In the 12th century, they were more or less exposed in the cliff face; the cave of the St. Aegidius Chapel was connected in 1170 with the so-called "habitaculum" of St. Rupert by the Holy Cross Chapel. The chapels of St. Gertrude and Maximus were probably not shaped architecturally until 1178, when Archbishop Konrad III added a dedication to Thomas à Becket, murdered eight years previously.

Abbot Balderich was also — in collaboration with the cathedral chapter, which later took over the work of construction — the initiator of that astounding technical monument, the canal tunnelled through the Mönchsberg to bring the water of the Alm into the town. Leaving St. Peter's Cemetery towards the Kapitelplatz, one suddenly hears the sound of rushing water; this is the Alm canal gushing out of the mountain. In 1136, the "artifex" Albert (an architect?) was commissioned to plan the tunnel. There is a possible connection between this construction, with the surveying involved in it, and a manuscript of the period (in St. Peter's) which contains, amongst other things, a "practical geometry", an "art of surveying". (The mediaeval copyist attributes it to Gerbert d'Aurillac, but in fact it dates back to land-surveyors of ancient times.) It is even probable that the original of this copy was procured on account of the impending construction work. Master Albert, whose freshwater canal must be numbered amongst the principal engineering feats of the 12th century, later entered the cathedral chapter as a lay brother, and could have brought the original manuscript with him.

Noteworthy monuments of the 12th century are also the tympanum of the south portal of the Franciscan Church and that of the Nonnberg Convent Church, neither of them in its original setting. The Nonnberg relief was used in the rebuilding of the church portal in the late 15th century, and the tympanum of the Franciscan Church survived two sets of alterations (early 13th and 15th centuries).

12th century Salzburg, after the eras under Virgil and Arno, was enjoying its second period of flourishing art and culture: fresh construction work and decorations in nearly all the churches, the goldsmith's art at its height, and monumental works of calligraphy and manuscript illumination. Then came the catastrophe of 1167, when a devastating conflagration reduced most of the churches to ashes. The cathedral and its two monastery buildings, the Church of Our Lady (today's Franciscan Church), St. Michael's Church, the cathedral baptistery, St. James' Chapel by the cathedral cemetery and the Church of Our Saviour on the right bank of the Salzach — all these were burned down. The "burghers' town" must also have suffered serious damage. Only the Monastery of St. Peter seems to have remained unscathed. Since at the 1166 Imperial Diet in Laufen the imperial ban had been imposed on Salzburg, and the Counts of Plain had thereupon cruelly oppressed the bishopric, they were held responsible for having started the fire.

The ruins of the cathedral remained standing for fourteen years, until reconstruction was at last begun in 1181, under Konrad III. In this same year, Nikolaus von Verdun completed his enamelled pulpit frontal in the monastery of Klosterneuburg, near Vienna.

The discovery of Virgil's grave in the south wall during the demolition of the old cathedral has already been mentioned. It caused a major sensation; miracles occurred at his grave, a history of his life was written, based on old records, and proceedings were instituted for his canonisation. This sudden wave of veneration for the former bishop of Salzburg proved highly advantageous for the building work on the cathedral; collections were organised and donations made. Virgil was canonised in 1233, and was promoted to Rupert's side as joint patron saint of the Province of Salzburg.

His remains were removed from the grave in 1288 and transferred to an altar. In 1315, Archbishop Wichard erected a new tomb (the slab bearing the inscription is preserved in the west wall of the south aisle in the Franciscan Church) which stood in the cathedral until 1599, when it was opened during the demolition of the building. Wolf Dietrich's biographer Johann Stainhauser writes the following account: "Anno Domini 1599, on the 18th day of January there was found during the dismantling of the altar of St. Virgil in the said cathedral church a stone coffin and therein one of copper and therein again a tin coffin, in which were the relics of St. Virgil together with a gold casket and some letters on parchment, of which hardly anyone could read or understand the script, and which Archbishop Wolf Dietrich sealed and took into his safe keeping." Later, in 1606, Wolf Dietrich had the relics removed unceremoniously to the sacristy of the Franciscan Church. In 1612, Marcus Sitticus arranged a solemn translation to the high altar of this church, and at the consecration of the early baroque cathedral in 1628, the relics, after their long peregrinations, were laid in a silver-mounted ebony casket in the table of the high altar.

THE CATHEDRAL BUILDING OF KONRAD III

Konrad III of Wittelsbach, the first cardinal to occupy the episcopal seat of Salzburg, had been, before his election, Archbishop of Mainz and Chancellor of State. He brought to Salzburg architectural ideas from the Rhenish imperial cathedrals, and the new cathedral building he initiated (using only the west towers from its predecessor) surpassed the old one in the concentration of architectural features such as towers and cupolas in the eastern part, and a quintuple nave. This cathedral was 110 metres long and about 50 metres wide; the vaulting of the centre nave rose to almost 30 metres, and the height of the tower over the crossing has been estimated at 49 metres. The architectural lines achieved the effect of reaching heavenwards; buttresses were necessary (as in Gothic building) to support the mighty towering vault. The quintuple nave (discovered during excavations), a feature generally reserved exclusively for Roman churches, occasioned contradictory interpretations. Here the reconstructed elevation must be taken into account. This shows the northernmost aisle to have been a row of chapels, not connected with the transept, but ending in an apse at the raised transept, under which was the crypt. The southernmost aisle was apparently separate from the church interior, and served as the northern side of the cathedral cloister. The new building was consecrated around 1200, and apart from minor additions in the Gothic period, remained unaltered until the advent of Archbishop Wolf Dietrich.

This urge to build heavenwards, to construct lofty towers, is a sign of a new philosophy of architecture which finds fulfilment only in vertiginous heights.

In 1223, the new Franciscan Church was consecrated, and the nave of this church is still standing. The pointed arches of the arcades already reveal Gothic ideas of form, even if the overall impression is still quite "Romanesque". This new style was received in Salzburg with reserve. Only in the capitals (in the side aisles) are there signs of new life stirring, reaching aloft and shaking off restraint. Leafage and calyces shoot forth, plant-stems curl their way through crockets, and even feathered creatures animate the clusters of foliage sprouting from the capitals.

The 13th century brought also alterations to the old Romanesque portals. In 1244, the old tympanum and lintel of St. Peter's were preserved in a new, higher splay, more

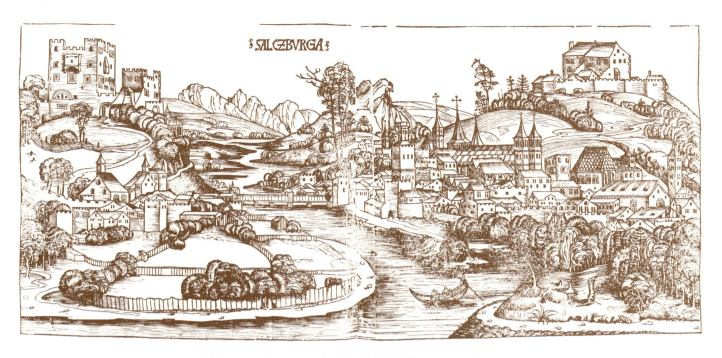

Salzburg around 1460. Woodcut by Michael Wolgemut, Nuremberg, 1493

angular and articulated. Round shafts alternate with slim octagonal pillars which in their turn divide to form stems and leaves in the capitals. The rounded Romanesque forms give way here to articulated lines and a liberated growth of leafage culminating in the capitals. The old "spiritual", stereometric and "artificial" forms are changed to conform with Nature, which is gradually being discovered in this century.

In this period of the Middle Ages, men read not the "Book of Nature", but books instead of nature, they studied not the world itself, but Plato and Aristoteles, not the heavens, but Ptolemy. Science observed not man, but what was written in certain books about man and the world around him. "Between ideas and objects there rose up, like a wall ever denser and more impervious, the mountain of texts, commentaries, and commentaries on the commentaries" (Eugenio Garin). The struggle to arrive at an understanding of nature through observation and experiment was to achieve breakthrough only during the Renaissance; the initial stages, however, took shape in the 13th century.

At this time, too, culture became independent of the monasteries. The monastery schools diminished in importance, and the leading role was assumed by the cathedral schools with their progressive, enlightened teachers, who were (also in Salzburg) learned, widely-travelled Dominicans — for "it was not the task of the monk to teach, but to mourn".

The canons, who lived in the cathedral monastery and taught in the cathedral school, brought new ideas into the parochialism of the town. A profound education had been available to them in the universities of Padua, Paris and Bologna. An old evaluation of these new educational establishments had it that "in legal disputes, Bologna arms the defenceless with the power of the law, while Paris dispenses in the arts that nourishment with which it nourishes the strong".

THE POWER OF REASON

Archbishop Eberhard II (1200—1246) had in 1218 accepted the newly-formed Dominican Order into the archbishopric and established them in Friesach. This was the new Order's first settlement in the empire. The Dominicans took over the preaching duties in the cathedral and the teaching in the cathedral school. Anselm of Canterbury's "sola ratione" (by reason alone) now came into operation; the newly-discovered rationality became the mainspring of the century. The clerics of the cathedral monastery brought the writings of their teachers with them from the universities of Italy and France, where they had either copied them or had them copied or merely illuminated. The scriptorium of St. Peter's declined; it lacked this stimulus, and St. Peter's was overshadowed by the new developments.

The belief in the power of reason and in the art of interpreting the law is illustrated by an example which seems to the modern unprejudiced observer, regardless of the Zeitgeist, merely curious and macabre.

Archbishop Eberhard II was one of the few ecclesiastical princes of Salzburg who took the side of the emperor (Frederick II), and he was therefore excommunicated, in 1239. Even when he died, in the care of "his" Dominicans in Friesach, the pope did not lift the ban, and he was given up to eternal damnation. The jurists of the Salzburg cathedral school, however, "armed" in Bologna, found a solution: Eberhard's dead body was sewn into a leather bag and hung up in the loft of the church in Altenmarkt! And there his mortal remains hung for forty-two years, until in 1288 he received absolution, and his body was buried in the vacant grave where Virgil had lain.

Behind this macabre "burial", there was a dry juridical rationalism whose subtlety had saved Eberhard from eternal damnation. Excommunication took effect as soon as the dead person came before the judgement seat; but the soul could do this only when the body had been committed to the earth. And this was exactly what had been avoided in the case of Eberhard, since his body hung between heaven and earth, and his soul, juristically safeguarded, could await absolution.

MYSTIC CROSSES AND THE "SCHÖNE MADONNA"

In the 13th century, mediaeval spiritualism had taken a fresh turn through the discovery of reason as a power which could lead to faith. Piety underwent a complete change in the 14th century, "when the solemn Gloria Patri of the Benedictines lapsed into silence . . . when people began to hurry away from the public service to a privately-dedicated mass in one of the many side chapels". Private devotions and private chapels belonging to the rich, privately-dedicated masses and artistically illuminated prayer-books are the expression of an "extra-liturgical" piety which seeks the path to Christ through the religious feelings of the individual. The Passion of Christ, which could be experienced through "compassion", and Christ himself ("through whose deathly pallor we were healed"), as a tortured wounded human being, awoke a deep religious sensibility. His royal crown had become a crown of thorns, the gold-edged coat a loincloth. The wound in his side was the object of superstitious veneration; theological treatises were written on the five wounds and the instruments of torture.

An essential item in any Dominican monastery was a crucifix with the figure of Christ represented as realistically and as cruelly tortured as possible. The one in the Dominican monastery in Friesach (dating from around 1330), with the body hanging on a Y-shaped cross (a lopped tree), is preserved in its original place, and an almost identical life-size mystic cross, originating from the old cathedral, hangs today in the Nonnberg Convent.

A further manifestation of this religiosity experienced with all the bodily senses was the desire for "show". The Eucharistic bread was no longer to be kept hidden in a pyx or a tabernacle; the holy presence should be manifest to all the faithful. Monstrances were now made, in which the consecrated host was exhibited for adoration. The festival of Corpus Christi also owes its existence to this religiosity.

The theme of the Passion, represented so realistically in the mystic crosses, gave rise to another kind of devotional image, the pietà. This is the sorrowful counterpart to the sweet, happy young mother of the "Schöne Madonna". During the decades around 1400, Salzburg was, next to Bohemia, the region in which these images of the "Schöne Madonna" were most widespread. Also ascribed to the area of Salzburg is one of the theological sources for Marian sermons and the new Madonnas, the so-called "Mariale", or Hymn to the Virgin. This 14th century theological treatise lays strong emphasis on the spiritual and physical beauty of the Virgin Mary, and stresses her part in Christ's work of redemption. Mary's complexion and the colour of her hair are described in detail. Another work takes six pages to portray her spiritual beauty and forty more to expatiate upon her physical charms.

The Romanesque-style Madonna held the Child, depicted as a tiny adult, on her lap, which represented the "throne" of Christ. The sculptors of the "Schöne Madonna" images show Christ as a child, with Mary holding him in the natural pose of motherhood, the Child reaching towards an apple or turning to face the worshipper. The grace and maternal joy, the realism and the "humanity" of these representations caused most of them to become popular miraculous images. Overlying the grace, even courtly elegance, of these figures is always, however, a painful presage of the Passion. Greatest joy is mingled with bitterest suffering; the "Schöne Madonna" and the pietà are the extremes of a religious experience whose almost unbearable tension is expressed in the visions of St. Birgitta of Sweden: "... As she wrapped him in swaddling clothes, she saw in her heart how his whole body would be torn with keen lashes ... and as she gently swaddled the hands and feet of her baby son, she could see how hard they would be pierced with iron nails on the cross ... thus she was of all mothers the most sorrowful, knowing of the bitter suffering he would endure".

The "Schöne Madonna" from the Franciscan monastery, exhibited in the Salzburg Cathedral Museum, dates from about 1410, and is said to originate from the archbishop's chambers in the Hohensalzburg Fortress. The figure grows out of the heavy folds of the mantle, which forms around the child a protective hollow further enhanced by folds cascading on either side. The mother's loving care is expressed by her hands, embracing the Child and holding out an apple for him, and by the head, inclined in loving contemplation. In an 18th-century niche in the north transept of St. Peter's Church stands a "Schöne Madonna", called "Maria Säul" because it originally stood on a column (Ger. *Säule*). The gilding dates from the Baroque period.

Archbishop Pilgrim II von Puchheim (1365—1396) was the ecclesiastical prince of most consequence in this century. Under his rule, the archiepiscopal court evolved an unprecedented splendour, the arts being held in high regard. Pilgrim increased the mining of silver and gold, which brought him a handsome revenue. Salzburg's development into an independent principality was concluded in this period, and the archbishopric reached its maximum territorial extent, including today's province of Salzburg, the Zillertal and the Brixental, plus Windisch-Matrei, and the 'Rupertiwinkel", with Laufen, Tittmoning and Mühldorf. Scattered possessions in Bavaria, Carinthia, Styria and Carniola (with the towns of Friesach, Leibnitz and Pettau) and, until 1405, also the princely *Probstei* (equivalent of a deanery) of Berchtesgaden, ensured extremely high revenues.

The archbishop of Salzburg held spiritual sway over the suffragan bishoprics of Regensburg, Passau, Freising and Brixen, and in the four proprietary bishoprics of Gurk, Chiemsee, Seckau and Lavant he had the authority to appoint bishops without consulting the emperor or the pope.

According to the fashion of the time, Pilgrim II founded in 1367, on the northwest side of the cathedral, his oratory for private devotions, and furnished it opulently with five altars and an organ. This chapel, in which Pilgrim was buried, was closed off from the north aisle of the old cathedral by a screen, and even had its own sacristy.

HEAVENLY AND EARTHLY LOVE

The society at the court of Archbishop Pilgrim consisted of learned canons and Dominicans, musicians and nobles, who cultivated sacred songs, but showed themselves by no means averse to earthly love, complaining, for instance: "We, fifteen courtiers, beg to inform the ladies that we are prostrate with lovesickness..." These songs have been handed down as the work of a "Monk of Salzburg"; we still do not know who is concealed behind this pseudonym, but in one song Archbishop Pilgrim names himself as the author. He laments the parting from a lady "E" in Schloss Freisaal (in Nonntal), where he had his summer residence: "The song is called the "freudensal" after a summer palace near Salzburg, and is composed in Prague ... I send the letter to the sweetest and loveliest woman in freudensal, the Most Honourable Lady ... write your answer to me, dearest E, to Pilgrim ..." Other names are mentioned, too, for instance one "master Johann, of the order of preachers", who could only have been a Dominican. It is taken as proved that the collection of songs stems from Pilgrim's circle of poets.

The love songs (Minnelieder) of the "Monk of Salzburg", which celebrate feminine charms and lovers' hopes, and the drinking songs are juxtaposed with the sacred songs and the hymns and sequences translated from the Latin, mostly in honour of the Virgin and Child. Sensuousness both religious and profane, love both heavenly and earthly, hymns to the Virgin Mary and love songs were practically interchangeable.

All these songs have been handed down along with their melodies. This is very important, because it was here that polyphony was first used in German songs. This *ars nova*, in which polyphony was achieved partly vocally (duets) and partly by instrumental accompaniment, necessitated a new, precise notation. This kind of music was a deliberate contrast to the anonymous monophonic *ars antiqua* cultivated in the monasteries, and may have followed examples from France and the music-loving court of Charles IV and his son Wenceslaus IV in Prague. Pilgrim had become acquainted with life at court in the papal exile in Avignon, where he had risen to the rank of papal chaplain, and he may have brought with him from there the "new art" of polyphony. Also, he frequently stayed in Prague, on diplomatic missions. A member of his retinue, the steward Reicher von Ettling, priest (plebanus) of Altenmarkt (Alten-Radstadt), acquired during one of these missions in Prague a "Schöne Madonna" (the so-called "Altenmarkter Madonna") and donated it to his church in 1393. One of the

"Monk's" best songs to the Virgin is dedicated to him, in the form of an acrostic, the initial letters of the lines reading "RICHERVS PLEBANVS IN RASTAT".

Besides mysticism and Virgin-worship, the 14th century brought the consciousness of charitable obligations, especially the care of the sick and the poor. The plague of 1348/49, the "Black Death", reinforced this movement. Leprosaria and hospitals were set up; the Bürgerspital (burghers' hospital) with St. Blasius' Church (at the end of the Getreidegasse) was founded in 1327, the church consecrated in 1350. The hospital wing, which still retains its 16th century form, now houses collections from the Museum Carolino Augusteum. The church is a simple, unpretentious building in the tradition of the mendicant orders. At the beginning of the 15th century, a gallery with its own altar had been built into the west part, to enable the ailing and the infirm to attend mass, and was linked to the "Gothic hall" and the hospital buildings.

HISTORICISM IN ST. PETER'S

Abbot of St. Peter's at this time was Otto II Chalchochsperger (1375—1414). The historical value of his architectural achievements has only recently been recognised, since the church vestibule, because of its "Romanesque" style, was for a long time dated in that period, with its bulky rib vaulting and its Roman windows. But it was in 1400 that Abbot Otto built this vestibule! A similarly anachronistic, even "historicist" style is manifest in the cloister he built. Finds from the Carolingian age and parts of Gothic buildings were used here, and these form, in conjunction with Gothic traceried windows, a peculiar conglomerate which one would hardly suppose to have been built as late as 1400. These historical fictions were deliberate on the part of Abbot Otto, who intended his buildings to awake memories of the venerable age of St. Peter's Monastery, through the use of parts of old buildings and bygone forms. This historicism presupposes a new understanding of "history", of the achievements of the past. It had nothing to do with an incapacity to build in a "modern" style, for right at the beginning of the 14th century, St. Peter's proved, with the Gothic chapel of the Virgin Mary (consecrated in 1319), that the monastery was entirely familiar with this new style. Neither was it due to lack of funds; these were not simply cheap building materials, but relics of old buildings, history-laden witnesses to a great past. Any observation judging purely on the grounds of style and chronological tables cannot do justice to such stylistic "flashbacks". The aesthetic principles behind such conglomerations of styles — which were nevertheless arranged with historical precision — have only become appreciated at their true worth in our age of "post-modern" architecture which readily uses examples from ages past. Abbot Otto's motive for this historicising style of building has only recently been discovered, and the publication of these sources will bring about a completely new evaluation of this architectural intention which was hitherto dismissed as "provincial" and "retarded".

"THE AUTUMN OF THE MIDDLE AGES"

Hardly had a generation passed since Abbot Otto drew on "Romanesque" forms to demonstrate the abbey's great age, when the citizens of Salzburg began building a "modern" late Gothic hall-church. Here the stylistic and genetic variance of attitude becomes evident, historicism being "modern" but using "old" and "out-of-date" forms, whereas the hall-choir of the Franciscan Church was designed to represent directly, without refraction through the past, the newly-awakened consciousness of the middle-class. The Franciscan Church was the parish church of the town; in contrast to the archiepiscopal cathedral, it was the liturgical centre of the bourgeoisie.

This example illustrates how, in a town like Salzburg, where such different and opposing, even competing communities as the bishops' court and the cathedral monastery, the Benedictine cloisters of St. Peter's and Nonnberg, and the bourgeoisie all had to coexist in a small space, each community sought expression in its own architectonic and artistic language. Although several centuries saw the coexistence of as many as six monastic communities, Salzburg was not a typical monastery town where people contemplated life through half-closed eyes. The fact that the archbishop was, from the late Middle Ages, also the prince, prevented the development of such contemplativeness. The bishops' court, which was also the administrative centre of the principality, with all the requisite "authorities", encouraged practical and realistic dealing. Revolutionary ideas or radical reforms never got anywhere. The old cathedral was the symbol of the bishops' power and a sign of its durability. The ancient monastery of St. Peter's, unable to compete with such power, attempted to establish clear indications of its seniority — even, if need be, in the form of a historical fiction or of documents fabricated "bona fide". These attempts included the building done under Otto II, Rupert's "rocky grave" in the church (said to date from the 14th century), and the *arcosolium* (a bench-like tomb) in the cave chapels, which was installed at the beginning of the 16th century to lend substance to the legends of the martyrs. In addition, the various rights, such as precedence and right of burial, which were energetically defended by the monastery, were taken as clear signs of seniority to the cathedral chapter, for seniority signified also priority.

Because of the specific structure of Salzburg society, it was some time before the middle classes became involved in this struggle for position. The citizenry was evolved on the one hand from the servant classes of the palatinate and the bishops' court, and on the other hand from the tradespeople who had settled at the "porta", the gateway to the ducal palace. The effects of this division are possibly still making themselves felt in various ways. Although the tradespeople no longer represent such a large proportion of the community, they are the ones who make an effort to "sell" the town's "image", according to their lights. The army of civil servants in the administrative offices of the town and the province has in our day, *cum grano salis*, assumed the role of the court servants. Whether the fact that Salzburg has more civil servants than other provincial governments in Austria may be attributed to tenacious court traditions, is not a matter to be decided here.

The little Rathaus (town hall) on the Kranzlmarkt, at the beginning of the Getreidegasse, became the seat of the town council in 1407. The architectural form is extremely modest; if one compares the puny tower with the others in the town, it is obvious that here it was not the citizenry that called the tune. In singular contrast to this was the enormous financial strength of the Salzburg merchants in the 15th century. They dominated the foreign trade market from Venice to southern Germany and Bohemia, and their aim was, understandably, to obtain "Reichsfreiheit" (being answerable only to the emperor) for Salzburg, after the manner of German towns. Emperor Frederick III granted them these privileges during the reign of a weak archbishop. Leonhard von Keutschach, however, who ruled the bishopric like a strict, often harsh paterfamilias, would tolerate no mutinous middle classes around him. So, on January 24th, 1511, he invited the town judge, the burgomaster, the town clerk and the privy council to breakfast in the Residenz. There he took his guests prisoner, reprimanded them severely, and had them taken to the Fortress and transported by night on open sleighs, despite the freezing cold, to Radstadt, where they were compelled to hand over Frederick III's charter and to renounce all privileges. This must have done permanent damage to the dawning self-confidence of the citizens. Even after secularisation in 1803, the Salzburg citizenry never really assumed a decisive role,

Tombstone of Ulrich Chalchochsperger († 1348) in St. Peter's.
Lithography by Peter Herwegen, 1867

and cultural initiative, as in the founding of the Salzburg Festival or the University, came from outside.

Let us return, however, to the 15th century, when the middle class, with its new-found wealth, planned the building of a modern parish church, financed solely by the citizens. In 1429, the merchant Ulrich Samer, for example, invested 12,000 gulden in the state bank of Venice, so that the interest could contribute to the building.

The first donations were made in 1408, possibly when preparations were being made; the actual construction was probably not begun until the 1420's. The original plan was perhaps to rebuild the entire church; the possible alteration of this plan, leading to the rebuilding of the choir and retaining the old nave, may have been made before 1432, when the architect, Hans von Burghausen, died. The early history of the church building is, however, not yet entirely elucidated. The originally intended "nonfinito" of the hall choir is also conceivable, for the Gothic period was often content with a new choir joined on to an older nave. This theory is also supported by the tendency of the period towards centralised design. The hall choir of the Franciscan Church, with its central pillar in the east, has the effect, especially as seen from the nave, of a hall developing radially around this east pillar.

There is, in addition, a "typological" argument for the original planning of the choir alone as a "centralised hall": before the late Romanesque basilica, a baptistery stood on this site, and canon law prescribed a circular form, a central hall, for this type of church. It is possible that Hans von Burghausen's hall choir represents a typological link with this baptistery. Later we shall see that Fischer von Erlach's altar may also hark back to old formal traditions of this place. Moreover, the existence of a baptistery here in the 8th century is also an argument for a pre-Virgilian cathedral building (for Bishop Johannes?) in the area of the later cathedrals, since baptisteries were usually situated to the west of the cathedral to which they belonged.

Construction of the hall choir progressed apace: in 1446 the triumphal arch was erected, and the walls had reached the base of the vaulting. A consecration of the altar is reported in 1449, and in 1460 the choir was completed by Stefan Krumenauer. The tower was erected in 1486—1498 to a design from Nuremberg. The pièce de résistance was an immense late Gothic winged altar, the work of Michael Pacher, who moved to Salzburg from Bruneck in 1484 in order to complete the great altar that was to be his major work. He died in Salzburg in 1498, and was probably buried in the small cemetery on the north side of the church. His grave is forgotten (the Residenz wings built by Wolf Dietrich cover the whole cemetery, apart from a tiny courtyard), and his mighty altar (estimated at a height of 16 metres) was destroyed at the beginning of the 18th century. Only the Madonna, considered a miraculous image, was included by Fischer in his altar, which is itself, of course, a masterpiece. One panel of the wing was used as a shelf in one of the sacristy cupboards; it is now along with two others in the Austrian Gallery in Vienna.

During the time he spent in Salzburg, Michael Pacher created the smaller St. Michael altar, which stood in the tribune of St. Michael's Church. At the beginning of the 17th century, when the tribune was pulled down, this altar was moved to the presbytery, and in the 18th century it fell prey to Baroque rebuilding.

The Franciscan Church, too, in common with so much in this town, derives its charm from an "art of arrangement" of heterogeneous forms. The side aisles are dark and vaulted, the main aisle narrow and almost without any independent source of daylight. A narrow and very high triumphal arch opens the view on to a bright Gothic choir, the extent and the height of which can, as seen from the nave, be only surmised. The greatest contrasts become apparent: while the late Romanesque nave with its solid walls and pillars, its weighty vaults and dividing bays, still gives an impression of straitness and confinement, the eye then rejoices in the bright spaciousness of the late Gothic hall choir with its atmosphere of width and freedom. The slender round pillars seem to grow aloft like tree-trunks, and the intricate network of the rib vaulting stretches overhead like a lattice of branches. The outer walls are pierced by great traceried windows; breadth and light dominate in this hall, expressing new religious life. It is quite possible that the Salzburg citizenry wished to document its new consciousness in this hall choir, which is placed in contrapuntal relation to the old nave. With this choir, the "laity", the citizens, "conquered" for themselves, as it were, the chancel; for in the older churches, in St. Peter's and the cathedral, a rood screen separated the laity from the choir, which was reserved for the monks and canons. The new hall choir, with the altar standing at its central pillar, "gathers" the congregation around this nucleus, under the spread of the vaulting which radiates from the pillar. Light floods in, washing around the slender pillars and bathing everything with equal intensity. In the old churches, the already strongly-defined hierarchy was further accentuated by the directing of the light, which did not reach into all corners of the interior.

The 15th century brought with it, after some initial crises, enormous progress in the arts. The Melk reform of the Benedictine monasteries, directed, amongst other things, against concubinage of priests and the general decline of morals, achieved great success in Salzburg. One result of the reform was the reorganisation of the old St. Peter's school. New buildings in the late Gothic style were the church of the Nonnberg Convent, the parish church of Mülln and the Chapel of St. Margaret in St. Peter's Cemetery. The art of

St. Peter's Cemetery and the Fortress.
Lithography by Albert E. Kirchner, 1838

manuscript illumination was once again cultivated; significantly, it was now priests or artists from the middle classes who undertook for St. Peter's the copying and illuminating of books. The "Grillinger workshop" produced magnificent specimens, around 1430; Ulrich Schreier made leatherwork bindings and illuminated the first printed books. Fragments remain of great altar-paintings, besides those of Michael Pacher, by Conrad Laib and Rueland Frueauf.

Only the Benedictine monasteries had been set back on the strait and narrow by the Melk reform, whereas the cathedral chapter of Augustinian canons and that of the nuns of the cathedral convent had hardly been affected. A covered passageway leading from the Residenz to the nuns' quarters, allowing the secular archbishops of the 15th century access to their mistresses, remained until Archbishop Leonhard von Keutschach had it pulled down, together with the concubines' quarters.

The serious political and financial problems the bishopric was experiencing at the beginning of the century were suddenly blamed on the Jews, and on 10th July, 1404, all the Jews in the town, with the exception of children under eleven and pregnant women, were herded together and publicly burned (along with, as it happened, sundry bonds . . .). Only a "magnus judeus" could buy his freedom.

The archbishopric reached rock bottom under Archbishop Friedrich V von Schaunberg (1489—1494). Although he was of noble birth, the chroniclers portray him as an idiot, hardly able to read or to perform his episcopal duties. Emperor Frederick III reviled him in front of his entire household in Wiener Neustadt: "This man is as much a bishop as a pig is a carrier pigeon. He can neither say mass nor read a schoolboy grammar."

In the 15th century, Salzburg was one of the wealthiest bishoprics in the West, surpassed only by Winchester. The electoral dues to be paid to the papal court after each election of a bishop were determined by the yearly income of the bishopric in question, and Salzburg was in the same category as Aquileia, Canterbury, York and Cologne.

Archbishop Leonhard von Keutschach (1495—1519) ruled with utmost thrift, and used the bishopric's resulting wealth to extend its territory. For the enormous sum of about 150,000 gulden, he purchased various feudal estates to round off the territory of Salzburg. He had to purchase with ready cash every privilege and every political concession from Emperor Maximilian I, who was chronically short of funds. What many of his predecessors achieved through diplomatic ingenuity, Leonhard could only attain by means of his well-filled cash-box. Even in the eyes of his contemporaries, he was a petty shopkeeper; the people irreverently called him "Liendl Wirt" (Leonhard the innkeeper) and "Pierschenk" (publican), because he had opened a taproom in the cathedral monastery, or "Liendl Ryebler", after the turnip *(Rübe)* in his coat of arms. But his rule was patriarchal; he had all the strongholds in Salzburg re-fortified, and reconstructed the Hohensalzburg Fortress according to the latest military recommendations, probably bearing in mind the peasant unrest of the preceding decades. He furnished the "Hoher Stock" (the castle keep) richly and splendidly, and these state rooms are amongst the finest secular Gothic rooms in Europe.

In 1502, solicitous of order in the community under his rule, Archbishop Leonhard had a "Hornwerk", (the "bellow", later named the "Salzburger Stier" [bull]) mounted on the townward side of the Fortress, a ". . . horn that is blown every day at four o'clock in the morning and seven in the evening, which makes a most agreeable sound". The strident F major chord issuing from 135 metal pipes was the "reveille" and the curfew for the people of Salzburg. (Appropriately enough, the notes F-A-C form the Latin imperative "do!") The Salzburger Stier, which was supplemented in the 16th century by a mechanical barrel organ, is the only surviving late Gothic "Hornwerk".

Late Gothic art in Salzburg shows an already familiar picture: a modest show of local handicrafts over against a whole display of works by foreigners. "The creative force came . . ., as ever, almost entirely from outside . . ." (Franz Fuhrmann).

CRIMSON STONES

One particular art form of this period merits closer consideration, since its raw material came from Salzburg: Late Gothic tombstone sculpture, which used red marble from Adnet, by Hallein. Salzburg examples of this art have been decimated; Archbishop Wolf Dietrich had the long row of bishops' tombs in the cathedral "shattered and crushed to pieces" when the old minster was demolished. The tomb of St. Vitalis, by one Meister Hans (1497), in the south transept of St. Peter's Church, is one of the finest monuments of its kind remaining in Salzburg. The monastery cloister, St. Margaret's Chapel in the cemetery, and the Nonnberg Convent still house other, simpler gravestones of red marble. These tombs, especially when they bear a life-size relief of the dead person, can be understood — like so much in mediaeval religious usage — as a last "imitation of Christ". For the use of this copper-coloured or crimson stone for a tombstone calls to mind the slab on which Nicodemus and Joseph of Arimathaea washed the body of Christ and anointed it with aloes and myrrh. This slab, variously called in the sources (esp. Niketas Choniates) the "lithos erythros", the "lapis purpureus", the crimson stone, the "Salbstein Christi", was a venerated relic in Ephesus. Emperor Manuel Komnenos I (1143—1180) had it brought to Constantinople, and after his death it was moved to the Monastery of Pantocrator. After the conquest of the town by the Turks in 1453, the slab was apparently offered for sale to the King of France, and has never been seen since.

The slab is said to have been coloured red for ever by the sacred blood of Christ, and the tears of the holy women fell upon it (according to reports) "white as milk" and "like drops of wax". Even this white-flecked stone was found in Adnet and named, according to the particular pattern of red and white, "Rotscheck", "Mandlscheck" or "Rottropf". These strongly mottled types of marble were used primarily for the tombs of kings and emperors — for instance in the grave of King Casimir Jagiello, by Veit Stoss, in Cracow (1492) and in that of Emperor Frederick III, by Niclas Gerhaert, in St. Stephen's Cathedral in Vienna (from 1468).

The deep significance immanent in the crimson stone (and its use as a gravestone), in which mediaeval man recognised the "copy", the "facsimile" of the sacred slab, enabled the dead person (according to late mediaeval conception) to participate in the Passion — his body, like that of Christ, lies on a crimson stone, bedewed with the tears of women.

A new age begins

RENAISSANCE IN SALZBURG

Archbishop Matthäus Lang (1519—1540) was descended from an impoverished patrician family of Augsburg. His friendship with the Humanists such as Konrad Peutinger dates back to his student years in Ingolstadt, Tübingen and Vienna; Johann Cuspinian later became his secretary. The Humanists always claimed Lang as one of their number. His early years were overshadowed by oppressive poverty; a chronicler later wrote: ". . . when he was young, he journeyed from town to town like any poor young student". His incredible career began when he entered the chancellery of King Maximilian I. In 1498 he had already become secretary of state, and been elevated to the rank of hereditary peer; thenceforth he called himself "von Wellenburg", after a castle near Augsburg. In 1501 he was promoted imperial councillor, and chroniclers go so far as to term him "half king", so great was his influence.

Lang's qualities as a diplomat were equal to any in Europe. He was overbearing and arrogant, a stern and unsociable man, regarded as a parvenu, and a realist politician of rare audacity. His contemporaries saw in him the completely unscrupulous assistant of Maximilian, "so very arrogant, more arrogant than the emperor"; he was the greatest "preferment-collector" of his time. He considered bribery an opportune means of achieving his ends, and wherever money was to be gained, he was to the fore. He collected one preferment after another, and by 1515 his income was estimated at between 50,000 and 80,000 gulden. Likeable traits are hard to find, apart from the fact that he was a great music-lover, and deeply interested in the sciences and antiquity.

Lang had been coadjutor in Gurk since 1501, and in 1505 he became bishop of this small proprietary bishopric in the diocese of Salzburg. In 1510, he was given Cartagena, in Spain, with the episcopal seat of Murcia as titular bishopric. In 1512/14 he achieved his ambition, when the pope appointed him coadjutor to Archbishop Leonhard von Keutschach, with the right of succession. The wealthy see of Salzburg would crown his collection of preferments. The cathedral chapter had supported this decision, and Lang promised in exchange secularisation, which would at last enable the canons to lead the longed-for "secular" life. In 1514, they finally laid down their monastic habits, and the cathedral monastery was dissolved.

Archbishop Leonhard had resisted in vain Lang's appointment as his successor, on the grounds that Lang would "prey" on the bishopric and bring it to financial ruin. In 1519, after Leonhard's death, Lang attained his goal of ruling as archbishop over the wealthiest (after Cologne) ecclesiastical principality in the German Empire.

Whereas Leonhard von Keutschach had been a typical representative of the Late Gothic period, under Cardinal Matthäus Lang the spirit of the Renaissance made itself felt in Salzburg. Symbolic of this was the installation, in the old cathedral, of a "horologium", an astronomical clock. "Time", a sacred reality in the Middle Ages, seemed almost rendered profane by this public display. We do not know whether this *horologium* had automatic mechanical figures with sacred motifs, but it certainly incorporated a perpetual calendar and an astrolabe as an "artificial universe" with more symbolic value than accuracy. The clock as a symbol of order and authority: this was quite in keeping with the Cardinal's self-confidence; but clocks were also a metaphor for the virtue of temperance, of self-control — not at all Lang's strong point.

As a humanist scholar, Matthäus Lang came to admire antiquity. In 1502, a time when even Rome had little to show in the way of antique art, a Carinthian peasant found on the Magdalensberg a life-size antique bronze statue of a youth, dating from the first century A. D. Lang, who was then still coadjutor to the bishop of Gurk, acquired the statue and later set it up in the Hohensalzburg Fortress. It seems that a bronze copy was made sometime during the 16th century, whereupon the original was taken to Spain. The copy remained in Salzburg until secularisation (1803), and is now preserved in the Kunsthistorisches Museum in Vienna. It is possible that Albrecht Dürer indirectly derived inspiration for his art from this figure. It was also Albrecht Dürer who drew a portrait of Lang and who designed a throne for the Cardinal in 1521. This throne, which was apparently never made, is a curious creation, more like a collector's curio than an article of state furniture. Lions and fabulous creatures are combined with architectonic fragments, helmet shapes and organic ornaments to form a "living", zoomorphic, delicate structural display which belongs less in the throne-room than in a procession of eccentric splendour.

Cardinal Lang's household in Salzburg is reputed to have been in "Renaissance style", the magnificent setting being provided by music and the decorative arts. From the sumptuous furnishings, there is preserved in the Museum Carolino Augusteum a Spanish carpet showing Lang's coat of arms in a laurel wreath. It was manufactured in Murcia, his titular bishopric in Spain, and dates from the years 1514—1519. The field with the coats of arms of the Cardinal and the principality is framed by Kufic letters and an "Arabic" woven band; Islam and Christianity are combined in this foreign fabric to magnificent effect.

Matthäus Lang was especially devoted to music, and maintained at his court an impressive company of musicians. The terms of a musician's appointment required him to play "violin, sackbut, flute, lute, and other instruments of music on which he can perform". At banquets, the positive organ was played first of all, then the flutes, and to conclude came the court singers and the fiddle-players. Paul Hofhaymer (1459-1537), the greatest composer of his time, of whom Paracelsus said that he was an artist on the organ as Albrecht Dürer in painting, was appointed at court by the Cardinal. A native of Radstadt, he lived in Salzburg at no. 18 Pfeiffergasse, not far from Paracelsus' house, and died there at an advanced age in 1537.

From a reign as long as Matthäus Lang's, one might expect an appropriate amount of building to have been undertaken. However, from 1523 onwards, the Cardinal had the greatest political and financial problems. The town was occupied by insurgents, and Lang had to conquer Salzburg at the head of an army of mercenaries. In 1525, rebellion against the ruler broke out afresh, and the insurgents occupied the town once more. Cardinal Lang was beseiged for three months in the impregnable Hohensalzburg Fortress, and only upon payment of a large sum of money was the army of the Swabian League prepared to relieve him. A further rebellion in 1526 was quelled, with great loss of lives. These wars cost Lang an enormous amount of money; even the church silver had to be melted down, and a major proportion of his income was pledged for years to come.

In 1517, Martin Luther had nailed his theses on the church door at Wittemberg, and the new teaching had rapidly attracted convinced adherents, also in Salzburg, especially in the mountain regions, amongst the peasants and the miners. Cardinal Lang, who was in principle not averse to it, soon

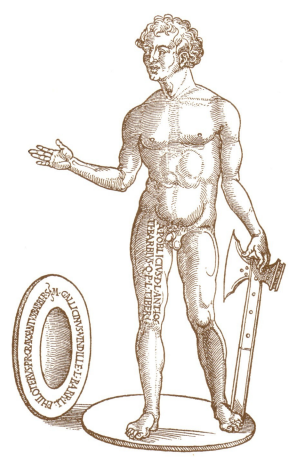

The "Jüngling vom Magdalensberg".
Woodcut, 1534

saw, however, the unity of his archbishopric endangered, and adopted an increasingly stern and inflexible attitude towards the Lutherans. He summoned to Salzburg Luther's friend and superior, the Augustinian Hermit Johann Staupitz. After Staupitz changed over to the Benedictine Order, he was until his death Abbot of St. Peter's (1522—1524). This period was characterised by a "widely diversified, active, partly turbulent, partly conservative evangelical Catholicism, which still permitted forms of thought and belief that could not withstand the later classification into separate confessions" (Heiko A. Obermann). During the Counter-Reformation, Abbot Martin Hattinger (1584—1615) had Staupitz' writings and Luther's letters to him burnt in the abbey courtyard, along with Lutheran books which Staupitz had purchased for St. Peter's Monastery.

The 16th century, an age which placed particular artistic

emphasis on the faithful portaiture of landscapes, has preserved for us, in two enormous views of the town (1553 and 1565), the Salzburg of the time just before Archbishop Wolf Dietrich's drastic alterations. These two great woodcuts (that of 1553 being a copy) are, apart from the view shown in Hartmann Schedel's *Liber chronicarum* of 1492 (showing the town in 1460), the principal pictorial sources of information on mediaeval, pre-Baroque Salzburg.

At the end of the 16th century, Salzburg still retained a decidedly mediaeval character; not one building exterior represented with any clarity the new architectural ideas of the Renaissance. Even the arcaded courtyard of the Bürgerspital (begun in 1556) reveals only in the almost endless rows of the repeated arcade motif the new trend in architecture, in which the repetition of specific units constitutes a façade governed by geometrical laws.

The new standard of living may perhaps have been more clearly perceptible in the decorative arts, such as that of the goldsmith, which could "assimilate" a new fashion more quickly, or in panel painting and the style of altars. Hans Asslinger's marble altar is preserved; it was erected in 1561 in the old cathedral, and moved in 1600 to the chapel directly behind the high altar in the Franciscan Church.

The Renaissance attitude of mind is probably most strongly reflected in the libraries of the educated laity, where the new literature often fell on more fertile ground than in the conservative monastic libraries.

A view of the town in 1553 shows a conglomerate of historical contingencies. Anyone looking for straight lines or a regular layout of open squares must see it as downright chaotic, a real labyrinth.

AN ARCHBISHOP'S "REMARKABLE URGE TO BUILD"

Wolf Dietrich von Raitenau (1587—1612) was only 28 years old when he was elected archbishop in 1587, by a majority of one. He was descended from a Vorarlberg family from Lochen on Lake Constance. His father was a colonel in the army of the emperor; his mother, Helene von Ems, was the daughter of one of the Medicis from the lower Milanese branch of that family, and Wolf Dietrich always liked to stress this relationship to the Medicis. There were also prominent churchmen in the family: Cardinal Karl Borromäus (d. 1584) and Cardinal Marco Sittico d'Altemps (d. 1595) were his uncles, the Medici Pope Pius IV (d. 1565) his great-uncle. Wolf Dietrich studied at the University of Pavia and was a pupil at the Collegium Germanicum in Rome, where he was brought up and educated. While he was still very young, his family obtained for him lucrative preferments in Constance, Basle and Murbach, and in 1575 he already held a canonry in Salzburg. His impressions during a journey to France and Spain in 1582/83 may well have shaped many of his later decisions on architecture.

As his secretary Johann Stainhauser reports, the young archbishop had "above all a remarkable urge to build". In the very year of his election, he had the "Trompeterschlössl" renovated. The following year, he bought up burghers' houses in the Kaiviertel and began work on the New Residenz, upon which the Glockenspiel was erected a century later. But the ceilings and the vaulting turned out to be too low, and so they were promptly pulled down again, along with the staircase ". . . and the archbishop took a dislike to the building, so that it remained in many things incomplete . . ." Very near this "newly-built ruin", a similar process took place. The chronicler Stainhauser shows pity for the felled "fine, full-bearing fruit tree that had stood in the garden". The building project fell through, and the garden remained devastated. In 1592, Wolf Dietrich had the wall surrounding the bishops' court (being also the wall of the cathedral cemetery) demolished and rebuilt nearer to the cathedral, together with a covered bridge linking the old Residenz with the New Residenz. But "the archbishop (for some unknown reason) took a dislike to it and had this building razed to the ground . . ." Amongst the people "there was no little murmuring", for the townsfolk had had to look on while the graves were dug up and the bones of their ancestors tipped into the Salzach. Hardly had they erected new tombs, at great expense, along this passageway, when these were torn down again. Thereupon the cemetery lay open and in ruins. Four years later, the passageway was rebuilt . . .

In 1597, Wolf Dietrich had the Alter Markt wing of the Residenz demolished, but the rebuilding very soon came to a standstill, and it was Marcus Sitticus who, years later, had the sorry remains cleared away. Wolf Dietrich had his brother Hannibal's newly-built palace on the (present) Mozartplatz pulled down in 1604, and until his enforced retirement in 1612, "the whole thing was left lying in a heap". Across the river, near the Palace of Altenau (later Mirabell), he had started building a pleasure-house with thick walls and pillars, but this project, too, was scrapped. The construction of a new stone bridge over the Salzach progressed up to the first pile, but then Wolf Dietrich's deposition put a stop to the work, and his successor Marcus Sitticus had it pulled down again. And a building in the "Frauengarten" (the present Festival precinct) "was abandoned, besides other secular buildings which it is unnecessary to enumerate". No comment is needed; Wolf Dietrich's legacy to Salzburg consisted of ruins and piles of rubble distributed throughout the town.

ARCHBISHOP WOLF DIETRICH AND VINCENZO SCAMOZZI

In 1589, two years after his instatement, Wolf Dietrich built on to the apse of the south aisle of the old cathedral a magnificent new sacristy with a monolithic marble pillar over five metres high. And in 1596 he built in the cathedral his mausoleum which, with its costly furnishings, is reputed to have used up something like 100,000 gulden. His private oratory was in the south transept, and was linked with the Residenz by a passageway inside the cathedral. It was in this oratory that a fire started in the night of 11th December, 1598, destroying the roofs of the cathedral but doing very little damage to the interior. "On account of this fire, there was amongst rich and poor much furtive murmuring against the archbishop . . . that he had by design . . . himself started the fire". This grave suspicion is probably unfounded, for Wolf Dietrich even made an attempt to restore the damaged vaulting; but the heavy layers of plaster on top of it, combined with heavy rainfall, caused it to collapse. In January 1599, work was begun on pulling down the altars and opening the bishops' tombs. These jobs took a remarkably long time; it was not until seven years after the fire — in the meantime, the bishops' tombs had been, with unprecedented impiety, "cleared out", and many of the tombstones shattered — that demolition of the walls of the old cathedral was begun in 1606 (only the bell-towers had been pulled down in 1599).

By 1612, the year in which Wolf Dietrich was forced to abdicate and was held prisoner in the Fortress, the foundations had been laid for a new cathedral building facing north. The façade was to have been linked by arcades with the Residenz and the New Residenz. This project, too, was left behind by Wolf Dietrich as a torso; Marcus Sitticus had the foundations dug up again, and started construction on the present Solari cathedral.

The final project for the north-facing cathedral had been preceded by extensive plans and planning alterations for the new building. The architect Vincenzo Scamozzi (1552—1616) from Vicenza, a pupil of Palladio and a wordy academic Late Mannerist, had drawn up plans for an enormous building, which was apparently, however, not to Wolf Dietrich's taste. Scamozzi spent the winter of 1603/4 (though perhaps he was here as early as 1599) in Salzburg,

Door console from Vincenzo Scamozzi's treatise on architecture, 1615

and seems to have had a decisive influence upon Wolf Dietrich's building concepts, which until then had looked somewhat aimless and desultory. At any rate, in 1604 Wolf Dietrich started demolition work on his brother's palace, which probably obstructed the view from the New Residenz over the Salzach to the Kapuzinerberg.

Scamozzi planned the alterations to the New Residenz (until then unfinished); he set out his ideas in a long-winded treatise: "And in Salzburg in the year 1604 we have recommended how to extend the new palace . . . with a long passageway from one corner to the other, and another in front of the hall to give a view down to the Salzach and over to the green hill [Kapuzinerberg] opposite . . ." (Grundregeln der Baukunst, 1678; *vide: Mirror of Architecture* . . . London, 1690). In the autumn of 1604, Wolf Dietrich bought several houses, with the intention of having them pulled down; during the 25 years of his rule, the number of such houses reached 55 — ". . . because of this, rooms and lodgings have become very expensive . . ."

Over the years, however, a certain system and purpose become discernible in all this chaos of building and altering. Indubitably, Scamozzi had taken over the planning of the "bishops' town" (perhaps even before 1603). "Cuttings" and open squares were hewn in the mediaeval labyrinth. In the Frauengarten, near the new stone quarry, the court stables were built (the site of the Grosses Festspielhaus). The monastery cloister built on to the south side of the Franciscan Church had to make way for the new road. Thus a second east-west thoroughfare developed, running from the Bürgerspital past the stables and the Franciscan Church to the cathedral, and continuing through the cathedral square and the Kapitelgasse into the Kaiviertel.

On the former site of the cathedral monastery is now the Kapitelplatz, and the cathedral cemetery had to make room for the Residenzplatz. The Mozartplatz has replaced a whole row of houses and Hannibal's palace. The Domplatz was already bordered to the north by the newly-built Residenz and to the west by the arcades; the garden "Dietrichsruh" (on the north side of the Franciscan Church) remained unfinished, as the gigantic pilasters in the Sigmund-Haffnergasse testify. The chapterhouses, the New Residenz, the court stables and the wing of the Residenz adjoining the Franciscan Church were the only buildings in the Old Town to be completed under Wolf Dietrich.

He alleviated to some extent the shortage of accommodation by building on the previously vacant *Salzachgries* (Gries=gravel) — today's Griesgasse. In the New Town, he had the "Trompeterschlössl" enlarged into a monastery for the Capuchin monks he had summoned, and in the garden landscape in front of the town walls he erected for his mistress, Salome Alt, the garden palace "Altenau" (later Mirabell), ". . . embellished around the outside with all kinds of herbs, trees and fruit . . ."

The transformation of the cathedral cemetery into an open square demanded a replacement; the cemetery of St. Sebastian, planned in the style of an Italian *campo santo,* was to house the graves of the citizenry. The strange thing was that only a year after he had erected, at vast expense, his mausoleum in the old cathedral, Wolf Dietrich began building a new one (the Gabriel Chapel) in St. Sebastian's (1597). It is quite understandable that his contemporaries wondered greatly at his desultory building activities.

GEOMETRY AS A FORCE OF ORDER

The building carried out at Wolf Dietrich's behest can scarcely be reviewed; it is difficult to establish an exact chronology, for hardly had he begun a project than he abandoned it to be continued at some later date. However, some basic features of his planning can be determined: his predilection for constructing thoroughfares (the road up to the Capuchin monastery, or the one through the "Gstätten" to Mülln), for streets and squares with architectural boundaries, for passageways and arcades. The new streets and thoroughfares created lines of communication between parts of the town which had previously had no connection with each other, and the geometrical structures brought order into the "disorder" of the overall aspect of the town. These thoroughfares gave rise to a stronger flow of traffic and of movement in general, felt to be necessary and liberating. The covered bridges (Franciscan Monastery, Mülln and the connecting passageway over the cathedral cemetery) guide the eye, as if from one stepping-stone to another, within the town. The wings adjoining the Franciscan Church are narrow, "passage-like", upon pillared arcades, altogether resembling bridges. The bridge motif of the cathedral arcades, too, probably derives from the arcades which were to have linked the north-facing cathedral, had it been built, with the other buildings.

In his building enterprises, Wolf Dietrich constantly fluctuated between feverish activity and sudden apathy. He must have been acutely susceptible to that insidious acedia, the state of melancholic stupor in which the "fountains of the spirit" dry up, and which emanated from this town with its "mustiness" and its lack of firm footing. Against this danger of the loss of a sense of order, he set his utopian plan for reconstructing the town; the chaos should be rendered "transparent" by mounting geometric structures to give the place perspective. However, he (or Scamozzi? — for when Wolf Dietrich was faced with remonstrances that he should not destroy "Virgil's" venerable cathedral, he is said to have replied laconically: "What do you mean, 'Virgil's' — it was built by masons'") drew no extended dividing lines through the centre of the town; the time was not yet ripe for the dashing, confident, endless straight lines which were later to become a hallmark of the Baroque age. The lines here are "refracted", interrupted, or at angles to one another, resulting in units complete in themselves, connected like links in a chain.

The "essence" of Salzburg is also discernible in the atmosphere of the squares, which are surrounded by smooth, inflexible surfaces. Blank walls dominate; the

The Domplatz. Engraving by Karl Remshard
after Franz Anton Danreiter, c. 1735

Ibex and lion, the coat arms of Marcus Sitticus and the archbishopric

Wolf Dietrich is often called the "Renaissance prince", but this age was in fact long past; the profound spiritual revival associated with it never took place in Salzburg. Wolf Dietrich was simply an absolute ruler who knew his Macchiavelli (he had even copied out several chapters of *Il Principe*). He erected palaces for his personal pleasure — the cathedral had to wait its turn. The palace for Salome Alt was completed within a few years, and so were the luxurious stables for his "fiery steeds". The horse was the symbol of passion; it was Archbishop Ernst Thun who first paid "monumental" tribute to the horse-tamer as a symbol of *prudentia*, able to dominate passion. But even Wolf Dietrich's noble steeds had only symbolic importance, for he himself was an indifferent horseman. During his flight from Salzburg, in October 1611, he had to stop for a day in Radstadt and again in the Lungau because of "swelling in the thighs". Without these halts, the soldiers sent by the Duke of Bavaria in his pursuit would never have managed to capture him.

The downfall of Wolf Dietrich can be told in a few words. The "salt war" broke out between him and Maximilian I, Duke of Bavaria, over the salt in the Dürnberg and in Berchtesgaden. The Bavarians had always been fond of posing as guardians of Salzburg, and Wolf Dietrich's occupation of Berchtesgaden at last gave them an excuse to intervene with military resources in the archbishopric. The "Great Elector", Maximilian I, a puritanical product of Jesuit education and a "dominating character of monkish seriousness", had long cast envious eyes on Wolf Dietrich's ruling power. He disapproved of the archbishop's "family life" and was extremely resentful of the fact that the Jesuits, so powerful in Bavaria, had until then been successfully kept away from the archbishopric. Moreover, Wolf Dietrich had not joined the Catholic League (1609), and the Duke saw this policy of neutrality as a betrayal of Catholic unity. When Maximilian advanced upon the town of Salzburg, Wolf Dietrich made a precipitate exit; he was captured, and after his resignation in 1612, was held prisoner in Hohensalzburg Fortress until his death in 1617.

Mönchsberg cliff and its relationship to the town are reflected here. The façades of the Wolf Dietrich period (the New Residenz, the arcades opposite the cathedral) are completely inflexible and sterile, their elevation almost like a projection of the drawing-board sketch. They lack "body" and weight; they are fitted together like thin panels. The "insubstantiality" of these façades, their impersonal sobriety, their cultivated severity all reflect a similar active concept of perspective, which can prevent the "sinking into melancholy and sloth".

Artistic activity can consist in the "revelation" of what already exists in nature, or else in a deliberate counterstroke to this. Wolf Dietrich, with the aid of Scamozzi, set his utopian concept forcibly and rigorously, as a formal regulative measure, against Salzburg's lack of solid foundation. Quite intentionally, he tore the town's character out of the imperceptible and unplanned course of history, and set it off along new lines of development.

CAPRICORN AND LEO

Archbishop Marcus Sitticus von Hohenems (1612—1619) was Wolf Dietrich's cousin, and like him had been brought up and educated in Italy. After Wolf Dietrich became archbishop, Marcus Sitticus succeeded him in the Salzburg canonry he had held. The relationship between the two is described as cool. Marcus Sitticus seems to have followed with great interest the dissension between Wolf Dietrich and the Bavarian Elector — eighteen days after the archbishop's flight, Sitticus was already in Salzburg. The cathedral chapter elected him successor by a large majority. The position he inherited was not an easy one; the Bavarian Elector demanded payment of the costs incurred by the war, and stipulated membership of the Catholic League; moreover, the archbishop was not to keep more of a household at court than was absolutely necessary. Also, Wolf Dietrich had been at first officially the prisoner of the pope, but now Marcus Sitticus had to assume responsibility for his predecessor's imprisonment in the Fortress. Until Wolf Dietrich's death, he lived in constant fear of being overthrown, and outlived his cousin by only two years.

In the years of his election, Marcus Sitticus appointed as cathedral architect Santino Solari (1576—1646), an Italian from the Intelvi Valley, by Lake Como. The foundation stone for the present building was laid in 1614. The building had progressed as far as the base of the roof, when Marcus Sitticus died in 1619; his epitaph reads: "hardly had the prince arrived at the roof than he had to descend into the vault".

The personality of Marcus Sitticus necessarily pales somewhat in historical records, for as successor to a man like Wolf Dietrich, he found few admirers for his pragmatic decisions. It is to him, however, that we owe the appointment of Santino Solari. Marcus Sitticus transformed the feverish building activity of his predecessor into a systematic process, always, of course, with a feeling of obligation to the vision of Wolf Dietrich. (Only by an age which embraced the cult of the genius could this be interpreted as a weakness on his part.) His successor Paris Lodron ruled the archbishopric for thirty-four years, whereas Marcus Sitticus had a mere seven years in which to put the town and its finances in order. He never did join the Catholic League, and he actually managed, by pleading the rebuilding of the cathedral, to postpone payment of reparation. As a wily tactician, he was certainly superior to Wolf Dietrich. He and Solari together must be credited with the creation of the cathedral, which Paris Lodron simply completed according to the plans as they stood.

Marcus Sitticus also built the unique Palace and Gardens of Hellbrunn, transplanting to the North the Italian-style "villa suburbana". He it was, too, who had Italian operas performed for the first time north of the Alps. And he must even be recognised as the founder of Salzburg University, for which he appointed Benedictine monks as teachers, instead of the Jesuits so influential in Bavaria. Since there were too few students, the new school at first took the form of a college; so in this case, too, Paris Lodron, with the for-

Organs with mechanical figures,
after Athanasius Kircher, 1650

mal inauguration of the University in 1622, had simply continued the project of Marcus Sitticus.

WATER, MUSIC AND MELANCHOLY

In 1613, in the spring following his election, Marcus Sitticus began work on the Palace and Gardens of Hellbrunn, on the well-watered Hellbrunner Berg to the south of Salzburg. The chief architect was most probably the cathedral designer Santino Solari. Italian sculptors, in collaboration with indigenous artists, created the garden statuary, and the entire park was completed in only two years.

Hellbrunn has to a large extent retained its Manneristic, early Baroque character; apart from minor alterations, the park has been spared modifications of the Baroque or Romantic periods.

To experience this garden properly, one must approach it from the direction of the Hellbrunner Allee (Avenue), which runs from Nonntal due south and is lined with villas and small palaces erected by the Salzburg aristocracy. Emsburg was built by Marcus Sitticus for his mistress, Barbara von Mabon, and Emslieb was the residence of a scapegrace nephew of the archbishop.

Following the avenue, the visitor is for a time uncertain where it is taking him, for the apparent direction is *past* the Palace; then right at the end, after a sharp bend, there stands the Palace, suddenly and unexpectedly, before him. This Manneristic principle of "surprise" is a leitmotiv of the whole layout.

In the main courtyard, in the grotto under the flight of steps up to the Palace door, another theme of Hellbrunn is introduced: Bacchus, in the shape of a water deity with two ibexes — the heraldic beasts of the archbishop. Hellbrunn is an aquatic "pleasure-ground" governed by Bacchus; here time flows by in diverting revelry, just as flowing water assumes a variety of forms.

The purpose of this "pleasure-ground" was "amusement therapy". For melancholia was at that time a fashionable and widespread ailment, to which the "nature" of Salzburg also contributed. To counteract this spiritual apathy and the danger of the "leaden" crippling depression, doctors recommended airy living-quarters, light wine, agreeable conversation and, above all, music, which, it was held, opened the "air-holes" — the pores of the body, through which the evil spirits would depart and the spirit of life could flow in.

The ibex in the grotto is a reminder of the builder; in the zodiac, it is one of the water signs (Capricorn), and belongs, together with tree and water spirits, to Bacchus' entourage. It lends its name to the ancient dramatic form of the tragedy (Greek *tragōidía* = goat song). Hellbrunn was also the scene of theatrical performances. Marcus Sitticus, a "singular amateur of pageantry and mummery", had brought to Salzburg the new Italian art of the "dramma per musica", the opera. In these works, dramatic poetry, music and scenic representation were combined to form a theatrical whole. Performances of the Italian operas "Orfeo", "Perseo" and "Andromeda" are reported from the years 1618 and 1619. Even if it is uncertain whether Monteverdi was in fact the composer of this "Orfeo", these were nevertheless the first performances of Italian operas in the German-speaking world, and thus the court of Salzburg had pioneered Latin theatrical culture in Germany. The performances perhaps took place in the "Steintheater" on the Hellbrunner Berg; here Marcus Sitticus had a quarry converted into a romantic natural theatre. These music dramas in the new "stile rappresentativo" had put an end to the old undefined, fluid unity of players and public. Through the distance separating audience and actors, the mythical action was elevated into the realm of the unreal, the magic. The play took on the appearance of a tableau, and could be fixed in sculptured and theatrical groups. Some of the mythological figures in the "water-garden" were certainly inspired by the archbishop's passion for the theatre.

Behind the Palace, among the grottoes, water-operated moving figures and fountains, are the still pools; is it the shining abode of the water-spirits we see in their depths, or only the reflection of the Palace? The visitor is kept in a constant state of nervous expectancy, now scared, now amused, alternating between light and shade as he escapes from the dark caves into the sunlight. But even out in the open he is allowed no peace of mind, for another shower may take him unawares, and he has to keep moving. There are plenty of places to suit a melancholy mood — springs and grottoes, where Neptune rules or Orpheus sings, where ibexes emerge from the water. It was supposed to be dangerous to fall asleep near a spring or a well, which were gateways to the Underworld; there is no risk of this here, for the trick fountains, like the water-spirits, are capricious, mischievous and cunning. Not even the reveller, overcome at last by wine and drowsiness, will find peace here, for the jet of water issuing from the stool he is sitting on recalls him promptly to the present moment. The fountains prevent the senses from growing numb, and set them free on the wings of laughter.

The water-operated figures were able to conjure up "artificial life" or "living pictures" before an amazed public. But these were costly pleasures; the Baroque writer Johann von Grimmelshausen warned against the realisation of such dreams: "But if you wish to make for the eyes as well as for the ears an extraordinarily wondrous amusement, such as is given in a theatre, then order to be manufactured for you the strange inventions of Athanasius Kircher, which will take more out of your purse than it will put dripping in the soup . . ." (*The Art of Becoming Rich*, 1672).

How very expensive these "toys" could in fact be was borne in upon Archbishop Jacob Dietrichstein (1747—1753), when he commissioned the "mechanical theatre", a view of the town with 256 moving figures in it. In the end, it cost three times the estimated sum, and the "mechanic" even had to be interned to make him complete the work after years of delay.

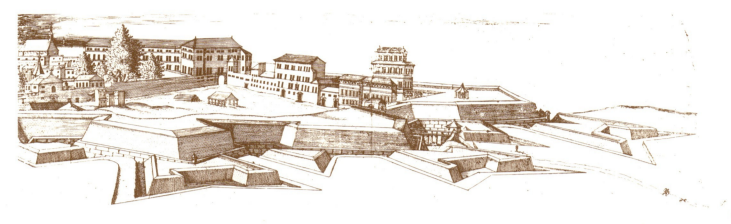

The fortifications in the Mirabell district.
Engraving by Philipp Harpff, 1643

SALT — THE SECRET OF A COMPOUND

In the great hall of the Palace, the walls of which are covered with illusionistic frescoes by Donato Mascagni (Fra Arsenio), appears the motto of Marcus Sitticus' reign: "Numen vel dissita jungit" (The might of a deity joins even that which is disunited). Ibex and lion, the heraldic beasts of the Hohenems family and the archbishopric respectively, embrace each other in heraldic illustration of the motto. But the figure can also be interpreted as an alchemistic allegory, as a "mysterium coniunctionis", as a secret of combination, for in the Zodiac these two signs — Capricorn (water) and Leo (fire) — are diametrically opposite each other, so can never meet. Only Christian alchemistic mysticism manages to bring the two together: "Two elements which fan the flames of an inexorable enmity between them, come together in a marvellous compound, in salt. For salt is all fire and all water" (Filippo Picinello, Mundus Symbolicus Lib. XII cap. XXVII, 260). Salt — Salz-Burg has achieved this apparently impossible union; but the salt was also considered as "lapis", the philosopher's stone, which was an alchemistic parallel for Christ.

The essence of alchemical thought was to free things from accepted associations and to unite them into new, unprecedented compounds. This urge to transmute was characteristic of the entire age, the alchemists forming within it only a specialised group, whose business it was to investigate the mysterious processes of transmutation. Marcus Sitticus' "transformations", his masquerades, his predilection for automata (machines brought to "life" through concealed motive power), his transmutation of nature into culture in the Steintheater — these represent the naive, courtly side of this desire for transformation.

PARIS LODRON — "PATER PATRIAE"

By a cunning policy of neutrality, Archbishop Paris Lodron (1619—1653) had managed to keep the spiritual principality of Salzburg out of the Thirty Years' War (1618—1648). In gratitude for the years of peace under his rule, the citizens of Salzburg bestowed on him in 1650 the ancient Roman title of "Pater patriae". He did not wish, either, to join the Catholic League, as the Bavarians vehemently demanded; Salzburg supported the Catholic princes only with a contingent of troops. The building of the cathedral progressed slowly, for Paris Lodron considered the fortification of the town to be the more urgent task; Salzburg "had been until then like an open village". The wall of the Old Town (from the Nonnberg to the Klausentor) was renovated and strengthened, Hohensalzburg Fortress had new barriers added, and the Mönchsberg was also fortified, especially in Mülln. A wall was built right round the Kapuzinerberg, the Franziskischlössl serving as quarters for the guards. But the most extensive fortifications were needed in the Mirabell district, for here the town had no natural protection, this was its most vulnerable side. Santino Solari, the cathedral architect, also engineered the archbishop's fortifications. He built a wall surrounding the Mirabell district, from the Kapuzinerberg to the Salzach, with all the latest constructions — bastions, ravelins and curtains. The art of fortification was at that time a form of applied mathematics related to geometry, and abstract mathematical rules dominated the literature on the subject. In those parts of Salzburg where "nature did not conform to art", comparatively simple walls were built, following the lie of the land — the art of fortification had to conform to nature. On the flat land of the Mirabell district, however, the whole science of "regular fortification" (of geometrical and utopian planning, far removed from military and economic reality) could be deployed in all its geometrising irrationality. These complicated types of fortification were more of a gesture of defence, a "bristling", than real, practical protection. In addition, the company of saints was then called upon to stand guard over the ramparts; each town gate was placed under the protection of a particular saint, the idea being that "where 'tis not God that guards the city tower, in vain is all the watchman's might and power" (Daniel Speckle, Architecture of Fortifications, 1589). Salzburg, thank goodness, was spared the proof of these installations.

SOLARI'S CATHEDRAL

Amid uproarious festivities lasting a whole week, the like of which Salzburg had never seen before, the cathedral was solemnly consecrated in 1628. While in Germany the Thirty Years' War was raging, while fear, poverty, hunger and death took their relentless toll, Salzburg celebrated with fireworks, open taverns and free food for the people. With a procession through triumphal arches, the relics of the patron saints, Rupert and Virgil, were carried to the new metropolitan church. "The Baroque age was still able to hold celebrations in comparison to which those of our time look paltry, where a few flags signify rejoicing, and the general public is kept at a distance by ropes and tickets of admission" (Franz Martin).

The massive gloomy walls of Solari's cathedral call to mind a stronghold — a divine stronghold. Leaving aside the façade, one is reminded of the Middle Ages, of great solid walls with unadorned windows cut in them, and of sombre vaults. The predominant building material is stone, "Nagelfluh" from the Mönchsberg. The rusticity of the squared stone, the *opera di natura,* is symbolic of the primitive forces of the earth. In these ashlar walls, art has re-created the Mönchsberg rock with its cave chapels and ennobled it with a marble façade. Although this cathedral was considered modern, it, too, like much in Salzburg, bears strong marks of the local traditions. On the one hand, Solari's walls conform to the sombre aspect of the mediaeval minster; on the other, the old cave chapels of the Mönchsberg rock offer an ever-varied theme. The "spirit of the Middle Ages" which is expressed by the building (apart from the façade), its almost "Protestant" simplicity — this is intentional, corresponding to a plan. The Counter-Reformation, the re-Catholicising of the Church, had been given its spiritual programme at the Council of Trent (1545—1563), and, in contrast to the Protestants, the Catholic Church returned to the mediaeval scholastic dogmas. New churches were to have the central hall as large as possible, without any divisions, and their atmosphere was to be created through the magical effect of light.

The marble façade is merely affixed like an ornament to the main body of the building, giving the effect of a costly setting for a venerated relic. The façade and the main body are not conceived as an organic unit in the architectonic sense; the cathedral is a conglomerate of concepts. The façade is a "triumphal wall", comparable to the triumphal arches of wood and canvas through which the procession advanced during the festival of consecration. The marble gives it durability and relates it to the main building behind; and the faithful, passing this grand frontage, see a solemn promise of the renewal of their faith.

The nave is a broad, barrel-vaulted, dimly-lit hall ending in a bright triple apse under the dome. While the nave receives only indirect daylight, the walls of the "clover-leaf" choir are pierced by 43 windows which flood it with light. The splays of the window reveals are emphasised to make more vivid the impression of the penetrating light, as in the words of Gregory the Great (pope, 590—604): "in the slant of the windows, that part where the light enters is narrow, but the inner part which admits the light is wide ... and so the windows are built to open so that grace can enter into the hearts of all that open them to receive it ..."

A PATRON OF THE NOBLE ART OF ARCHITECTURE AND FOUNTAINS

Archbishop Guidobald, Count of Thun (1654—1668) also contributed considerably to the realisation of Wolf Dietrich's vision of a "Rome of the North". He was "a sympathetic amateur and very great patron of the noble art of architecture and fountains". With the "gallery" to the south and the marble "bridges" of the arcades, he gave the cathedral square that intimate completeness which makes it the "atrium", of the cathedral. The character of this square varies between the sacred and the "merely" solemn; it is indeed the ideal setting for the performance of "Everyman", the "Play of the Life and Death of the Rich Man", in which sacred and profane are mingled.

The completion of the cathedral façade with the octagonal towers in 1655 and the building of the arcades was marked by a letter of congratulation: "The basilica now stands complete; he has joined it to the palace with marble constructions on both sides . . . the holy place and the princely residence are one house".

Architect of the cathedral arcades was probably Giovanni Antonio Dario, who, like Solari, came from the Intelvi Valley by Lake Como. The arches are crowned with heads of wild horses and the window frames with eagles' heads, an allusion to Guidobald's heraldic beasts, unicorn and eagle. Salzburg is a town in which one is deposited by the flow of time like alluvial sand or gravel on a river bank — here time sweeps no-one along with it. But sometimes a water-spirit will emerge from the streams or the watery shallow ground to remind the town of its origins. The "Wilder Mann" on the fountain in the Hofstallgasse, erected in 1620 on the "Gries", the gravelly river-bank, as a container for live fish, must have risen from the Salzach as a river-god with dripping wet locks, and been tamed into an escutcheon-bearer of the town. It was a prophetic river-god, too, who revealed to the people here the whereabouts of the salt deposits — but that must have been a very long time ago, when the Salzach still bore its ancient name, "Ivarus".

Snorting steeds spring forth from the watery fissures of the Residenz fountain; on the amorphous stone heap, crawling with water reptiles, primitive giants, rooted in the stone, hold up a basin of fine, clearly-sculptured lines. Dolphins, attracted by the music of men, balance above this a shell-like basin with a triton, from whose conch-shell trumpet the fountain springs triumphantly. This "most famous Salzburg water-fountain" was erected in 1656—1661. The sculptor may have been Tommaso Garuo Allio, who was Dario's brother-in-law and came from Scaria in the Intelvi Valley. (It has been established that he was in Salzburg during the years 1656—1658; he later worked in Italy, and died before 1676).

In the 1950's, a twelve-sided "corset" of paving was laid around the base of the fountain, isolating it from the surrounding gravel and destroying the natural relationship, so that the horses no longer look as though they were breaking loose in all four directions, but are simply puffing ineffectually.

All the building enterprises of the 17th century were dominated by Italians: Elia Castello (the Gabriel Chapel), Andrea Bartoletti (St. Sebastian's Cemetery), Vincenzo Scamozzi, Santino Solari, Giovanni Antonio Dario, Tommaso Garuo Allio and Gaspare Zuccalli (St. Erhard's, St. Cajetan's) are the most important among a great number of Italian architects, masons and stuccoers who worked in Salzburg. It was the "Latin" century, à la mode not only in Salzburg; the "Austro-Italians" left their mark on buildings in the Habsburg lands, too. Not all of those active in Salzburg were outstanding artists, but the idea of the bishops' town as a work of art created and assembled over generations lent support to the weaker among them.

FISCHER VON ERLACH AND SALZBURG

In 1687, Johann Ernst Thun (1687—1709) was elected archbishop. He was averse to everything Italian, and immediately dismissed Gaspare Zuccalli, although the Church of St. Cajetan was not yet completed. Italian masons were also no longer required in Salzburg; only the Italian stuccoers were kept on, since it was more difficult to find replacements for this skill. Ernst Thun's policy in the arts was anti-Italian; "his man" was an Austrian, the young Johann Bernhard Fischer.

What explanation is there for this change of idea which brought to an end the age of Italian architects, not only in Salzburg, but in the whole of the Habsburg Empire? The defeat of the Turks in 1683 had brought people to a new awareness of the Empire. The victorious defence action and the repulsion of the Turks into the Balkans had increased the desire for ostentatious self-representation, and the "German" faction at the Viennese court gained enormous influence. If, up to 1680, the court had not sought personal reflection in its architecture, which had always consisted simply in appropriate housing, providing a suitable background, now came the new era of symbolic, illustrative architecture. The Italian architects were not equal to this task, however; architects were required who could offer

The Collegiate Church.
Engraving after Aemilian Rösch, c. 1707

more than "architectonic Mannerism", who would put their skill at the service of the new spiritual climate. Out of a synthesis of the great Italian and French architectural systems, whose ancestors were the historical (especially the antique) architectures, and out of a consideration of its own building traditions grew the architecture of the High Baroque. Fischer von Erlach was the first to formulate this synthesis; he accomplished the decisive change of style from Austro-Italian to Austrian Baroque, establishing the "Kaiserstil" which was to remain dominant in the architecture of the German-speaking countries until 1740. In his church buildings in Salzburg and in the altar of the Franciscan Church, the theological roots of the new style of ecclesiastical architecture are for the first time manifest.

When Johann Bernhard Fischer (he received the title "von Erlach" in 1696) was appointed, shortly before 1690, by the newly-elected Archbishop Johann Ernst Thun, to act as his adviser in building matters, the framework of the town's development had already been laid down; but during the twenty years or so when he was active in Salzburg, Fischer did far more than merely fill the architectural gaps.

Up until that time, the main thoroughfares and the major church buildings lay parallel to the river. By building the Collegiate Church at right angles to this traditional alignment, Fischer managed to place a new landmark in the panorama of the town. The dome of the Collegiate Church is, so to speak, the pivot which takes up the line of vision from the cathedral and directs it via the northerly façade over to the New Town. There it is answered by another of Fischer's buildings — Holy Trinity Church with the Priests' House. These relationships, this confrontation, across the river, of two dominating architectures and their incorporation into the existing lines of vision have animated the aspect of the town and "dramatised" in the High Baroque manner the gentle flow of early Baroque planning.

Fischer carried out another successful and highly original plan by fitting his Church of St. Mark into an awkward site. The large area reserved for the church and convent of the Ursuline nuns lay at the north-west end of the town, at the Müllner Tor (Mülln Gate). By placing the church at the narrow end of the area, opposite the town gate, Fischer created a ceremonial entrance for visitors coming from Bavaria; the church, high and narrow, divides the stream of incoming travellers like the prow of a ship. The towers, set back behind the façade, introduce on the one hand the narrow Gstättengasse by the cliff, and on the other the Griesgasse on the bank of the Salzach. The gateway and the church façade form the poles between which the atmosphere of the square is created. This idea of placing a church façade opposite a gateway is not new to Salzburg, for around 1600, Scamozzi planned the gates of the arcades over the Franziskanergasse to be opposite his immense cathedral.

The main parterre of the Mirabell Gardens dates back to plans drawn up by Fischer around 1688. The line of its axis extends across the river again, to the Old Town and the Cathedral. Also, his ornamental horse-pond on the Sigmundsplatz (in its original version, before Franz Anton Danreiter rebuilt it) was "animated" by the confrontation of triumphal portal and horse-tamer. The portal, with its frieze of arms, atlantes and personifications of Europe and Asia, was intended as a reminder of the glorious part played by a contingent of Salzburg cavalry in the battle against the Turks in 1683. In the frieze of arms there appears an ensign with the letters SPQS (Senatus Populusque Salisburgensis — the senate and people of Salzburg), in imitation of the ancient Roman SPQR. This was of course merely an amusing historical embellishment, for Ernst Thun (like Max Gandolph Kuenburg, 1668—1687) was an absolutist ruler, and the "senate and people" of Salzburg had no competence to make decisions, but merely to receive orders and to increase the fame of the archbishopric in the struggle against the Turks.

Another work (though not officially ascertained) by Fischer was the conversion, in 1692/93, of the quarry on the side of the Mönchsberg to a summer riding-school. Fischer was at that time in charge of all the building being carried out, and the gallery in the rock "is such a magnificent idea that it could hardly have sprung from the brain of a Salzburg civil servant" (Franz Martin). "But to incorporate this open 'Theatrum Equestre', unique in the whole world, as permanent scenery in a conventional theatre is unforgivable" (Hans Sedlmayr).

THE ALTAR AS A FOUNTAIN OF LIFE

The theological origins of Fischer's church architecture first became apparent in his Salzburg works; the high altar of the Franciscan Church illustrates theological concepts and the formal traditions of its setting. In 1708, the Franciscan Monastery decided to pull down Michael Pacher's splendid Gothic winged altar, and to replace it with a new work. Only the miraculous image of the Virgin Mary was to be re-used in the new altar. Fischer von Erlach submitted a design, and in 1710 the altar was completed.

As mentioned earlier, in the 8th century there had been a baptistery on the site of St. Mary's (now the Franciscan) Church. The archetypal centrality of this baptistery probably decided the similar tendency of the Gothic hall choir. This motif is taken up once more in Fischer's altar, which stands like a small circular temple beneath the central pillar of the choir. The altar shows also, however, an unmistakable typological relationship with representations of the fountain of life in Carolingian evangeliaries (e. g. the evangeliary from Soissons). As in those pictures, the richly-ornamented diadem arches high above the columns, but the rear half of the entablature is curved downwards — the altar is also meant to be seen as a "fountain" surrounded by columns. The font, too, represents this "fons vitae", and Rupert von Deutz (d. in c. 1130) and Alcuin of York called the Virgin, in a hymn, "fons vitae": "for in thee is the fount of life". The theological significance of the baptistery and the Church of St. Mary, of the baptismal water and of the Virgin as the "fountain of true life" has been condensed in Fischer's altar into an imagery rich in associations, whose archetypal motifs reach far back in history.

In his "Plan of Civil and Historical Architecture"... (London, 1730), Fischer made a comprehensive documentation of his interest in historical forms. He demonstrates architectures from the history of mankind in five books, in more than eighty engravings. His own creations stand at the end of this imposing series, which begins with a description of the Temple of Solomon. In 1712, he had intended to include European buildings by the "Goths" — mediaeval architecture.

The steep proportions of Fischer's Collegiate Church may also have been inspired by mediaeval architecture; "here Greek and Latin traditions are combined, and the interior has a touch of the mediaeval" (Erich Hubala). This church is also dedicated to the Virgin, to the "Immaculata Conceptio", which, although it had not yet been dogmatised, the professors of the Benedictine University of Salzburg advocated on theological grounds and confirmed in a solemn oath in 1696 (the year the foundation stone was laid). The Mariological programme influenced the entire building; the monumental columns in the presbytery are an allusion to the two pillars of the Temple of Solomon, the Virgin herself being seen as the "Temple of Solomon", the "house of wisdom". This cross-in-square church is the university church of Salzburg; in the angles between the arms of the cross are four chapels, dedicated to the four patron saints of the university faculties.

Next to the Emperor, it was Archbishop Ernst Thun who gave Fischer the most commissions. Such industrious building demanded a thrifty distribution of funds, and so Fischer's buildings employ modest resources; marble was used sparingly, and the corridors in the buildings were paved only with planks and cobblestones. But it is not costly materials that make these buildings impressive; what amazed the people of Salzburg was the "extraordinary inventiveness" that produced such unprecedented forms. The Collegiate Church seemed to his contemporaries so revolutionary and unfamiliar that in 1701 someone wrote in a student album: "If an aged German of such a building should catch sight, he'd not know where he was — it would give him a real fright."

During the construction of his building projects in Salzburg, Fischer von Erlach visited the town only occasionally, and the work was supervised by local overseers. Thus it easily happened that, in many instances, the work of the masons took precedence over the artistic design. Examples of this are the central pavilion of Klesheim Palace, where the open arcades were closed and given smaller windows, and the oval windows at the top of the towers of the Collegiate Church, which were apparently, contrary to the original plans, walled up from the start. The weather (frequent rainfall) may have been the reason for this; but in fact Salzburg had never favoured copious fenestration — unbroken wall surfaces were more in kepping with the inhabitants' attitude to life. (So many projects in Salzburg have been "rained off", or rather, "watered down"; a modern instance is the roof of Wilhelm Holzbauer's St. Virgil cultural centre, which bears little resemblance to the architect's original plans).

Archbishop Ernst Thun had distributed his fortune for the erection of religious buildings, with instructions that after his death the appropriate parts of his body should lie there: thus his brain was interred in the University Church, his heart in Holy Trinity (to which it was closest), and his viscera in St. John's Hospital Church.

Thun's successor, Archbishop Franz Anton Harrach (1709—1727), had a different protégé — Fischer's archenemy, Johann Lukas von Hildebrandt, who was prepared to hasten to Salzburg immediately after Harrach's election, but was restrained from doing so on the grounds that Fischer was still there, and "it was not a good idea to have them both together".

Archbishop Harrach commissioned works in Salzburg from other artists who worked for the Emperor's court in Vienna and for the nobility there; the painters and frescoers Johann Michael Rottmayr and Martin Altomonte and the sculptor Raphael Donner all worked here. Harrach had the state rooms of the Residenz decorated and furnished in a uniform style; the cycle of paintings on the ceiling, portraying scenes from the life of Alexander the Great, is an allusion to the lordly virtues and the wise government of the Prince-Archbishop. In the "Schöne Galerie", Hildebrandt designed a richly-framed niche above the fireplace for the bronze statue of the "Jüngling vom Magdalensberg"; two plump cherubs flank the base and admire the youth's classic beauty.

The Mirabell Palace also underwent alterations under Harrach; Hildebrandt combined the Manneristic arrangement of separate buildings, dating from Wolf Dietrich's era, to form a uniform four-winged building with a tower in the east wing. Unfortunately, the Palace was severely damaged in the great fire of 1818, and it was reconstructed in the unexciting style of a municipal building. The staircase, aside from the main axis and too narrow, does not conform to the Baroque ideal; Hildebrandt had to take into account the distribution of space in the previous building — but he nevertheless achieved a charming result. A vital element of its individuality is the rich and ebullient ornamentation of the staircase. The laborious business of climbing stairs suddenly becomes fun, when accompanied by the billowing motion of the stone waves with cherubs sporting on their crests. One is borne along, so to speak, on the upsurge of the tide. Hildebrandt made alterations in the gardens, too; the "Zwerglgarten", with its statuary of deformed dwarves, and the "Heckentheater" (hedge-theatre) date back to the years 1713—1717.

FORCIBLE TAMING

Archbishop Leopold Anton Firmian (1727—1744) declared immediately after his election that he did not look upon the throne as an easy-chair, but as a weaver's stool, for a ruler is like a weaver who has many strings to hold . . . This zeal was soon felt by the Protestants in the archbishopric. Since the 16th century, severe measures had frequently been taken by the Counter-Reformation, in the country districts, and under each archbishop small groups of Protestants had left the land for reasons of faith. But up to that time, no ruler had taken all too rigorous steps, since the emigration of the industrious Protestants, the farmers and miners, would have been highly detrimental to the economy of the principality. Under Firmian, the catastrophe came about. An overzealous chancellor and some intolerant missionaries managed things with such ineptitude that many Salzburg Protestants were prepared to emigrate rather than renounce their faith. The Prussian king's offer to take in the emigrants brought about a real wave of enthusiasm, and in the end some 20.000 Salzburgers left the archbishopric in 1732. This mass emigration caused a sensation throughout Europe. (Decades later, Goethe was moved by it to write his epic poem "Hermann und Dorothea"). Most of the emigrants settled in Eastern Prussia, smaller groups went to Holland, and forty-two families found a new home in Ebenezer, Georgia. The economic damage sustained by the archbishopric was enormous; decades were to pass before the farms could be inhabited and cultivated once more.

In the university, too, there was unrest. In the so-called "sycophant dispute", the students complained that what the professors served up to them was ". . . old second-hand goods, rubbish and vapour. Since no-one but themselves reads their books, they extol these themselves. They take no notice of any other books." This problem was solved by pensioning off the old professors or sending them back to the monastery. The university's reputation was altogether

The court stables and horse-pond.
Etching by Franz Müller after August F. H. Naumann, c. 1795

bad at the time — it was so deeply in debt that a public announcement was made to the effect that no-one was to lend any money to it.

Archbishop Firmian had Fischer von Erlach's ornamental horse-pond (on the Sigmundsplatz) rebuilt, and erected the one on the Kapitelplatz, with the chronogram "LeopoLDVs prInCeps Me eXstrVXIt" (Prince Leopold built me), which reveals the date of construction, 1732. The supervisor of the episcopal gardens, Franz Anton Danreiter, designed this structure, which links mountain and fountain by the outline of its ornamental wall. In this same year, Danreiter rebuilt the horse-pond of the court stables; the "backdrop" wall, with its central motif of the triumphal arch, frames the group of hourse and tamer, which was then for the first time displayed on a raised pedestal. The Neutor behind, leading through the Mönchsberg to the Riedenburg district, was constructed in 1764, and the portals were decorated in 1767 by the brothers Wolfgang and Johann Baptist Hagenauer.

The political and allegorical significance of the horse (and its tamer) in the Baroque age is clearly demonstrated in these two horse-ponds. Monarch and realm, ruler and subjects found themselves mirrored allegorically in the image of the horse and its tamer or trainer. That age, which thought constantly in terms of analogies and images, saw religious and political correlations, a "theology" of the horse, confirmed by passages in the Bible. Such words as "Behold, we put bits in the horses' mouths, that they may obey us; and we turn about their whole body" (James 3/iii) authorised the prince to "tame" his subjects, and to "keep a tight rein on them". A strong character, fortitude and restraint of passion (the horse was *the* symbol of passion) made up the ideal personality of the age. That it should be none other than Archbishop Firmian, who brought endless suffering upon his subjects, who had these horse-ponds built in 1732, the year of the Protestant expulsion, seems paradoxical, almost like providing an alibi. For the ideal of the relationship between rider (tamer) and horse, of the relationship between a prince and his subjects, was harmony; sympathy with the horse was considered analogous to the love of God as the Creator of animals. Christoph Pinter von der Au expressed this in 1688, in the verses: "He who loves the horse according to God's will does not abuse the beast, but trains it with great skill!" Sympathetic "taming" was the ideal of the age, and not forcible measures.

PRINCE-ARCHBISHOP FIRMIAN — "THE TIMEPIECE OF THE LAND"

In the introduction to this book, Archbishop Firmian's passion for clocks has been mentioned; in his bedroom alone, he had six of them, including a luminous night clock and one with a celestial globe. The Scottish-born Benedictine monk Bernhard Stuart, who taught mathematics and astronomy at the university, had to calculate and design for the archbishop many mechanical clocks and sundials, which the court clockmaker, Jakob Bentele, then constructed.

This passion, shared by Firmian with other princes of the time, originated less in a desire for reliable and exact timekeeping than in the deeper significance of the clock. It was a symbol of order and authority, a metaphor for the relationship of the prince to the state, to his subjects. It was an allegory of the absolutist state based upon a central authority. There are many treatises from the Baroque age on the allegory of the clock; the prince is the "motor", the "balance-wheel", the subjects are the wheels, kept in ordered motion.

Christoph Lehmann wrote, in his *Florilegium politicum* (1630): "A prince and ruler is the timepiece of the land, all men are guided by him in their work as they are by the clock in their daily life." The Spaniard Diego de Saavedra Fajardo carries this analogy still further in his work *Idea de un principe politico christiano* (1659): ". . . Monarchy differs from other forms of government in that here one man alone gives orders, the others obey . . . Therefore a prince should be not only a hand in the clockwork of government, but also the balance-wheel, which sets the pace for the other wheels to move."

The clock was for Firmian a symbol of his authoritarian concept of order. The Protestants did not fit into this "state-clockwork"; they were wheels which were not right for the mechanism, and which upset the workings of the "state machinery". Horse-tamer and clock as metaphors for absolutist monarchy create between Firmian's clock mania, his horse-ponds and the expulsion of the Protestants an unexpected yet logical political and allegorical connection.

WOLFGANG AMADEUS MOZART

Leopold Mozart was born in Augsburg in 1719, and came to Salzburg in 1737 to study at the Benedictine university; only a year later he gained his baccalaureate in philosophy. But then his zeal appeared to wane; he was expelled from the university for non-attendance at lectures — one assumes that he devoted more time to playing chamber music with his friends than he did to his studies. He entered the household of the senior canon of Salzburg as a chamber musician, and three years later he became fourth violinist in the first violin section of the court *Kapelle*. In 1747, he married Anna Maria Pertl, and in their apartment on the third floor of no. 9, Getreidegasse, their children Maria Anna Walpurga ("Nannerl", 1751) and Johann Chrysostomus Wolfgang Theophilus ("Amadeus", 27th January 1756) were born. Leopold Mozart, who had in 1758 been promoted to second violinist, gave the children music tuition, and in Nannerl's music book we find entries such as: "Little Wolfgang learned this minuet when he was only 4", or: "Wolfgang learned this minuet and trio on 26th January 1761, the day before his 5th birthday at half-past nine in the evening, in half an hour."

Both children were very musical, but Wolfgang's talent continually amazed his father. His hearing was so sensitive that until the age of ten he had an insuperable fear of the trumpet; ". . . if you even held up a trumpet in front of him, it was just as if you had put a loaded pistol to his heart". Once the court trumpeter Andreas Schachtner, a good friend of the family, at Leopold's bidding blew his trumpet before the child, and Wolfgang very nearly fainted: "Hardly had little Wolfgang heard the resounding tone than he became pale and began to sink to the floor."

The reigning Archbishop Christoph von Schrattenbach (1753—1771) treated the Mozart family with great benevolence. In 1763 he appointed Leopold deputy *Kapellmeister*, and repeatedly gave him permission to accompany his children on concert tours; the sum of 600 gulden, which he donated towards their first journey to Italy in 1769, is entered in the account-book with the remark "for the little Mozart boy". The archbishop was a kind-hearted philanthropist; in Salzburg there was a saying: "D'Kinder, d'Narren und d'Hund liebt unser Sigismund" (The children, the fools and the dogs all love our Siegmund).

The child prodigy Wolfgang Amadeus and his sister Nannerl made lengthy journeys throughout Europe. In 1762, they performed in front of the Empress Maria Theresia, and from 1763—66 they travelled via Paris to London. The proud father wrote enthusiastically to his Salzburg friend and landlord Johann Lorenz Hagenauer, ". . . what he knew when we left Salzburg is a mere shadow compared to what he knows now. He exceeds all imagination." Wolfgang Amadeus was then eleven years old. In Bologna, he became a member of the Academia filarmonica (1770), and further travels in Italy followed immediately afterwards.

Meanwhile, serious changes had taken place in Salzburg.

The house where Mozart was born, in the Getreidegasse. Etching, c. 1828

The good Archbishop Schrattenbach had died, and his successor was Hieronymus, Count of Colloredo (1772—1803), a dispassionate and punctilious archbishop, who forbade his employees to travel, refused all applications for leave, and dismissed father and son Mozart at short notice. Leopold was immediately reinstated, it is true, but the easy-going period under Schrattenbach was past, and the Mozarts had to realise unequivocally that they were simply court servants. The final showdown between Archbishop Colloredo and Wolfgang Amadeus took place in Vienna. During an audience on 9th May 1781, Colloredo called Wolfgang a knave and a rascal. "Still filled with gall", Wolfgang wrote to his father in Salzburg to tell him of the altercation: (Archbishop) ". . . there is the door, mark you, I wish to have nothing more to do with such a (wretched knave) . . . at last I said . . . and neither do I wish anything more to do with you . . ." At this point, a lackey is said to have kicked Mozart out.

Wolfgang Amadeus returned to Salzburg only once more, to visit his family in the "Dancing Master's House" on the Makartplatz, where they had been living since 1773, and where Mozart composed some hundred works, including sacred music such as the *Credo* Mass, the *Organ solo* Mass and the *Coronation* Mass, numerous church sonatas, litanies and vespers, as well as sonatas, symphonies, minuets and serenades, and the operas *Il re pastore*, *La finta giardiniera*, *Idomeneo* and *Zaide*.

Mozart had high hopes for his career in Vienna — commissions from the nobility and the court, and above all a permanent situation. He exchanged his circle of family friends in Salzburg — his father's orchestral colleagues Johann Ernst Eberlin (1702—1762), Johann Michael Haydn (1737—1806), Anton Cajetan Adlgasser (1728—1777) and Dominicus Hagenauer, the Barisani family Robinig and Schidenhofen — for new ones in Vienna. These, however, stayed by him only as long as he was successful, and gathered together for a jolly evening's card-game only when he had money to gamble. Not one of them accompanied him on his last journey, to St. Marx Cemetery on 7th December 1791; his wife Constanze sought his grave in vain 17 years after his death, and was indignant that his resting-place had been forgotten. In the year of his death, he completed the *Magic Flute;* the summer-house in which he is said to have composed parts of this opera was brought from Vienna to Salzburg, and is now on view (as part of a guided tour) in the bastion garden behind the Mozarteum.

In 1801, Nannerl returned to Salzburg, after the death of her husband, Baron Johann Baptist von Berchtold zu Sonnenburg, chief of local government in St. Gilgen. She died in 1829, but wished on no account to be buried in the family vault in St. Sebastian's Cemetery, since she had never been on close terms with "the Webers" (Mozart's wife Constanze and her relatives) and Georg Nikolaus Nissen, Constanze's second husband. She is buried in the communal vault in St. Peter's Cemetery. Constanze also moved to Salzburg, in 1820, and in the year the Mozart monument was unveiled and the first musical festival was held (1842), she died, and was buried beside her second husband in St. Sebastian's Cemetery. The International Mozart Foundation was established in 1870, and in 1880 the International Foundation Mozarteum, still extant, was constituted. The music festivals of this institution were the forerunners of the Salzburg Festival.

Salzburg loses its independence and becomes a province

The Napoleonic wars and the concomitant redistribution of power in Europe put an end to Salzburg's independence. The chronicle of events makes it clear that the years 1800—1816 (the final union with Austria) signify the most crucial point in Salzburg's history. During this period, the town was despoiled of almost its entire collection of art treasures; what was not plundered or melted down was taken away by a succession of masters — the Elector, the French, the Bavarians and the Austrians.

The town was first occupied by the French in 1797 and 1800; Archbishop Colloredo fled to Vienna in 1801, never to return to Salzburg. In the peace of Lunéville (1801), it had been decided to secularise the archbishopric and to give it to Grand Duke Ferdinand of Tuscany in compensation for the land he had been forced to hand over to the infantes of Parma. Salzburg became an electorate, along with the principalities of Eichstädt, Berchtesgaden, and part of Passau; Archbishop Colloredo resigned in 1803, and Ferdinand III of Tuscany took possession of his new territory. This state of affairs lasted for just under three years, for with the treaty of Pressburg Salzburg became, for the first time, Austrian. Dominicus Hagenauer, Abbot of St. Peter's, indicates the reaction of the people of Salzburg thus: "What universal consternation this unexpected news spread about, can hardly be described. And who can hold this against us."

Months earlier, Duke Ferdinand, who this time had received in compensation the new electorate of Würzburg, had had all the valuables belonging to the archbishopric packed up and transported to Würzburg in droves of wagons. The incredibly rich archiepiscopal treasure, too, made up part of the fat "inheritance" raked in by the Grand Duke after a mere three years' rule. The treasure is now in the Palazzo Pitti in Florence.

The first period of Austrian rule lasted only from 1805—1809, but it was long enough for the choice items from the archives, art collections and libraries of Salzburg to be removed to Vienna. Everything the French had not requisitioned in 1800 was lifted *en bloc* by Viennese officials and taken to the imperial capital. Even the white deer from the game reserve in Hellbrunn had to move to Vienna. Salzburg's new status as a provincial Austrian town was received with dismay by the people. "Commerce is at an end, because there is no longer a ruler, nor a court, nor any employment, the money that comes in no longer goes into circulation, but has to be diverted to the capital . . ." laments Abbot Dominicus Hagenauer. War broke out again in 1809, bringing the return of French and Bavarian soldiers who had already overrun the town several times, the Bavarian hussars being "even more relentless than the French". In the peace of Schönbrunn, Salzburg was once more separated from Austria, and after a period of administration by the French, became a Bavarian province (1810—1816): "At this news there was universal consternation in the town."

The people of Salzburg have never felt akin to the Bavarians; the traveller Kaspar Riesbeck, who visited the town during the reign of Archbishop Firmian, writes of its relationship to its western neighbour: "About the national pride prevalent amongst these people, I do not know what to say . . . The inhabitants of this town become greatly annoyed if one calls them Bavarians . . . They wish to have nothing in common with the Bavarians, whom they consider far beneath themselves. One has to allow that the Salzburgers have rather better taste and manners, and rather less bigotry than the Bavarians; but to make so great a difference, and to place the Bavarians lower even than animals — that must be attributed to a powerful spirit of fantasy."

During these years, the Bavarians cleared out anything worth having that the privy councillors from Vienna had overlooked. At last, in 1816, Salzburg finally belonged to Austria; with great military ceremony, the Bavarian coat of arms was removed from the Residenz and the New Residenz, and was replaced by the two-headed eagle of Austria, to the loud applause of part of the crowd gathered on the Residenzplatz. 122 years later, the enthusiasm on the Residenzplatz applied to a quite different annexation.

View of Salzburg from the Mönchsberg. Lithography by K. Libay
after Johann Fischbach, c. 1848

Salzburg station. Lithography by Lohninger, 1860

THE ROMANTICS DISCOVER SALZBURG

In 1816, Salzburg had been demoted to the status of an insignificant "Kreisstadt" (the equivalent of a county town); the Salzburgers were not even granted the privilege of administration, since Linz, the capital town of the province of Upper Austria, had been given the competence for the administration of Salzburg, which had to wait until 1848 before it was made an independent crownland. The vicissitudes of the years following secularisation left in the cultural and economic structure of the town a vacuum which remained noticeable for about a century, until the establishing of the Salzburg Festival in 1917.

Salzburg was a sleepy little provincial town, hardly any bigger, with its 16,000 inhabitants, than it had been in Wolf Dietrich's era. Time seemed to have come to a standstill; no building was being undertaken, trade was exhausted, and the great buildings of the former archiepiscopal court, the Residenz and the New Residenz, were empty and "cleared out" — the last items of furniture were publicly auctioned. People looked back to the glorious past, for the future held no promise; they regretted the age when the archbishop's court had offered employment, and the great building projects opportunities to earn a living.

The Romantics, too, indulged in retrospection; they discovered Salzburg as a "picturesque" town, in which the past was preserved through chance events of history. Their paintings show the time continuum, the transition of atmosphere according to the time of day; Salzburg was the ideal place to become absorbed in history, to seek after the beginnings and the original forms of community life. The village-like character of the town and its environment, which had been merely pushed into the background by the lordly architecture of the archbishops, came into its own once more. The "farmhouses" around St. Peter's Cemetery were a favourite motif, or the shepherdesses on the Mönchsberg against the background of the town's architectonic splendour. In the Romantic paintings, goats graze on the banks of the Salzach, boats carrying salt float serenely downstream, and the unregulated river washes the tanners' houses on the Steingasse. The impression is one of a calm and leisurely age.

THE EMPEROR'S GIFT

With the building of the Vienna-Munich railway in 1860, "modern" dynamic ideas had come to Salzburg. The political conditions for the freedom of the citizens had been created in 1848, and Salzburg now wished to embark upon enterprises which would give expression to the community consciousness. The city fathers turned their attention first to the north — to the station, the railway, the mode of communication that embodied the new age. In this direction the town was to be extended, and towards Schallmoos. The walls, ramparts and gates of the fortifications were felt to be constricting, a hindrance to the free-flowing traffic which was a symbol of a dynamic economy. The prohibition of the erection of any new building in the area of the fortifications was revoked in 1860. On 1st May, 1866, to mark the 50th anniversary of Salzburg's inclusion in the Austrian Empire, the Emperor Franz Joseph I presented to the tain areas on the outskirts of the town contrasts blatantly with the beauty of the Old Town; while here commissions composed of arbiters of aesthetics lay down every detail of a window casement, in the outer districts blocks of flats designed to house thousands of people are erected solely in accordance with the laws of profit.

SALZBURG AND MODERN ARCHITECTURE

It may seem surprising that after the Second World War, it was the Church that found its way to realising projects in modern architecture. The parish church in Parsch (1953—56) and St. Joseph's College in Aigen (1961—64), both designed by the "Arbeitsgruppe 4" (Holzbauer, Kurrent, Spalt) were milestones in the architectural landscape of Salzburg. The parish centre of St. Vitalis (1967—72) and the St. Virgil cultural centre (1968—76), both by Wilhelm Holzbauer, made an impressive continuation of this succession of ambitious architectural projects. One can only guess at the reasons why the town and the province were not capable of such vision; this level of thought was probably lacking in the requisite planning, and would anyway have been eclipsed in the morass of party politics, individual interest and profit margins.

In recent decades, there has been much talk of building "in keeping with the Old Town"; just what this means is illustrated by a block of houses in the Griesgasse. Façades with a pitiful veneer of history give a flagrant demonstration of incapacity to comprehend the architectonic structure of the town. But unfortunately the Salzburg commissions still seem to be more readily convinced by bits of stone carving or wrought iron than by a structure truly "in keeping" with the town, without any historical frippery. Wilhelm Holzbauer has achieved in his buildings (St. Virgil and the Faculty of Natural Science in Freisaal) a "Salzburg" motif which fits organically into the architectural whole: the "alley-shafts" which, analogous to the narrow lanes of the Old Town, form the lines of communication in his buildings. In these glass-roofed "alleys", which run the full length and height of the main body of the buildings, are the staircases and galleries, in which the specific Salzburg atmosphere is revived, albeit in modern guise.

Beside this structural reference to an architectural motif typical of Salzburg, the stone carvings on the Natural Science Faculty building look somewhat superficial. This is a "maniera Salisburgensis", as Holzbauer himself calls it, but unfortunately based on a fiction, since the "Nagelfluh" stone was originally always whitewashed, although this is

Natural Science Faculty, galleries around the foyer.
Drawing by Wilhelm Holzbauer

town the ramparts from the Kapuzinerberg to the Mirabell Gate.

The ramparts, gates and wall were demolished to make room for the expansion of the town, and the building materials were used to regulate the Salzach, thereby creating fresh building sites on the banks. The "opening up" of the town to the north, in the Mirabell and Andrä districts, had made expansion possible, but had also led to the danger of faceless built-up areas. The ensuing history of the building undertaken in this area has demonstrated that it is not enough for a town expansion programme to fix a layout of roads and building plots and to erect a few "representative" buildings, when beyond that there is no concept to lend support to architectonically weak constructions. Concentration on the incomparable ensemble of the Old Town has never allowed the marginal areas into the focus of serious planning — until too late. The ugliness and bleakness of cer-

The Small Festival Hall. Drawing by Clemens Holzmeister, 1937

still not recognised in Salzburg. The wish to do justice to the stone has even caused the stone reveals of the newly-restored Collegiate Church to be left bare — contrary to the findings of the building commission. The Salzburgers have always had a penchant for bare stone; perhaps it gives them subconsciously a feeling of something to hold on to?

SALZBURG AS A "STAGE"

Since the days of Marcus Sitticus, the theatre has played an important part in Salzburg's cultural life. Kaspar Riesbeck (already quoted above) writes: "People have such a passion for the theatre here, that they crave the coming of a troupe of strolling players as they would in remotest Siberia the return of spring". Even today, Salzburg hankers after the coming of musicians, actors, conductors, television personalities and visitors, to bring "life" into the town — though perhaps in a rather different sense to that of earlier days . . . The concept of the Salzburg Festival was an offshoot of the Mozart festivals. The idea took shape as early as 1906, but it was not until 1917 that the "Festspielhausgemeinde" was constituted in Vienna; the champions of the new idea were Franz Schalk, Richard Strauss, Max Reinhardt, Hugo von Hofmannsthal and Alfred Roller. The novelty of their concept lay in the idea of holding musical and theatrical events in the open squares and courtyards of the Old Town; the Festival should be held not in an isolated theatre or concert hall, but in the unique setting of the town itself. It may well be that the architecture, the history and the ambience of Salzburg "cry out" for such a *mise en scène*. Secularisation had, after all, created a kind of vacuum; the splendid edifices were left standing unused or were converted for other purposes. Theatrical and musical events would, for a few days at least, bring life into those venerable walls and revive something of the spirit of the town's cultural past. Religiosity was rediscovered in ancient theatrical guise — the initiative behind performances of sacred plays came from a deep interest in pagan myth and Christian Mediaeval and Baroque faith. The Festival pioneers saw the theatre as something allegorical and metaphysical which could best be realised in those squares and courtyards which had been the scene of real history. The Cathedral façade was chosen as the backdrop for *Everyman* — authentic and impressive, since the scenic element was inherent in its very construction. Serenades in the courtyards, minuets in Hellbrunn — in Salzburg, one had only to stage local history, to produce old plays in their original settings, and one had a festival to offer, the success of which depended simply on the readiness of the audience to enter into the spirit of things. It is not easy, especially in our day, to keep an idea like this alive; financial considerations and columns of figures to be added up stifle all too quickly a noble concept.

The "scenic" character of the town is constantly at our disposition, with its façades like stage flats with little "body" to them; is it not a strange thing, then, that the performances are increasingly held indoors, that remarkable settings such as the Felsenreitschule are forced into the pattern of a conventional theatre? It is difficult to come to terms with the spirit of Salzburg; perhaps one succeeds more readily in the artificial atmosphere of stage machinery and backdrops than in the town itself. The lack of firm foundation, the "suspension", the leaden ambience of Salzburg demand constant movement, the therapy of music and theatre, rather as in bygone days incessant dancing was prescribed to counteract a poisonous snake bite. Theatre, music and movement are the appropriate measures to counteract the "sickness" of this town, the "morbus austriacus" diagnosed by Jean Améry, who considered Salzburg to be specially affected: "But since Austria, and specifically the border area around Salzburg, as a landscape, a townscape and a homeland hang, as it were, *in vacuo* — for what are they? German territory? Austrian? — one dangles with them in a ghostly no-man's-land, which is politically, socially and nationally indefinable".

St. Peter's Monastery kindly gave permission for the photographing and illustration of the capital on page 100, and most generously placed at our disposal the models for the illustrations on pages 95 and 133. The Chief Curator of Salzburg, Walter Schlegel, was kind enough to provide the model for the illustration on page 119, and the architect Wilhelm Holzbauer obliged by drawing the "Gallery" on page 138. The museum Carolino Augusteum let us have the photographs for the illustrations on pages 107, 131 and 137. The photographs for the pictures on pages 95, 119 and 133 were taken by Bruno Smetana, and those on pages 100 and 122 by Werner Schnelle. We should like to express here our thanks to all those who so willingly lent us their assistance in obtaining material for the illustrations.

A selection of specialised works on Salzburg is listed in the German-language edition of this book: "Salzburg — Die schöne Stadt."

CONTENTS

Salzburg — A Contradiction	5
Reflections on the "essence" of Salzburg	6
Salzburg between rock and river	6
"You are ruled by the shade"	7
Genius loci	8
COLOUR PLATES	9
The Origins of Salzburg — Early Monasticism	89
The rock is a refuge — petra refugium	89
St. Severin	90
The itinerant bishop Hrodpertus	91
Ecclesia Petena — Aquileia and Salzburg in the Dark Ages	93
Virgil from Ireland	94
Archbishop Arno — Salzburg becomes a metropolis	97
Virgil's cathedral, sacred books and the Tassilo chalice	98
Power and asceticism — the greatness of Salzburg and its flourishing monastic culture	103
The Cathedral Building of Konrad III	106
The power of reason	107
Mystic crosses and the "Schöne Madonna"	108
Heavenly and earthly love	109
Historicism in St. Peter's	110
"The Atumn of the Middle Ages"	110
Crimson stones	114
A new age begins	116
Renaissance in Salzburg	116
An Archbishop's "remarkable urge to build"	118
Archbishop Wolf Dietrich and Vincenzo Scamozzi	119
Geometry as a force of order	120
Capricorn and Leo	122
Water, Music and Melancholy	123
Salt — the secret of a compound	125
Paris Lodron — "Pater patriae"	125
Solari's cathedral	126
A patron of the noble art of architecture and fountains	127
Fischer von Erlach and Salzburg	127
The altar as a fountain of life	129
Forcible taming	130
Prince-Archbishop Firmian — "The timepiece of the land"	132
Wolfgang Amadeus Mozart	132
Salzburg loses its independence and becomes a province	135
The Romantics discover Salzburg	137
The Emperor's gift	137
Salzburg and modern architecture	138
Salzburg as a "stage"	139